21590

BOOKS BY
CHARLES E. RICE

Freedom of Association

The Supreme Court and Public Prayer

THE VANISHING
RIGHT TO LIVE

THE VANISHING
RIGHT TO LIVE

An Appeal for a Renewed

Reverence for Life

CHARLES E. RICE

1969
Doubleday & Company, Inc.
Garden City, New York

Grateful acknowledgment is made to the following for the use of their material which is reprinted with their permission:

Judge George H. Barnett for letter to the Association for Study of Abortion, 12/8/67; Al Capp for cartoon from "Li'l Abner," 1/6/68, "News Syndicate, Inc."; *The Medical Moral Newsletter*, September and October, 1967 for quotes by Drs. F. H. C. Crick, Joseph W. Goldzieher, Allan C. Barnes and A. W. Andison; Professor Norbert J. Mietus for quotes from The Therapeutic Abortion Act—A Statement in Opposition, page 16; Queen's Printer, Ottawa, Canada, for quotes by the Honorable Guy Favreau in Capital Punishment; Scepter Publishers for quotes from *Morals, Law & Life*, by Cathal B. Daly; Stein and Day Publishers, for excerpts from *The Wolfenden Report*, copyright © 1963 by Stein and Day Incorporated; *The New York Times* for quotes from the July 30, 1968 issue, copyright © 1968 by The New York Times Company; *Triumph Magazine* for quotes from an Editorial June, 1967; *U. S. News & World Report* for quotes from the article "The World's Biggest Problem" in the October 4, 1965 issue; Jerry Vogel Music Co., Inc. for lines from "Heaven Will Protect The Working Girl" from *Tillie's Nightmare*, by Edgar Smith and A. Baldwin Sloane, copyright © 1938.

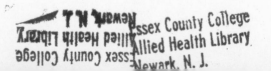

To Mary and our children, John Laurence, Mary Frances, Anne Patricia, Joseph Patrick, Charles Peter, Jeanne Elizabeth, and Theresa Helen.

I am grateful to John and Teresa Pando for their invaluable comments and suggestions on the substantive treatment of the issues involved; to Professor Robert M. Byrn, whose insight and background information were most helpful, particularly on the abortion problem; to Miss Audrey Soracco and Mr. John Delaney for their generous and thoughtful editorial assistance; to my mother, Mrs. Mary C. Rice, for her essential comments on the entire manuscript and her aid in the preparation of the Index; and, most important, to my wife, Mary, for her patience and indispensable help in developing the basic ideas and the manuscript.

Also, I acknowledge my indebtedness to Mrs. Michael Suchy, whose typing of the manuscript was characteristically accurate and prompt and whose suggestions on content were a great help; to Miss Patricia Kossmann for her efficient aid in processing the manuscript; and to Mrs. Agnes Ciaffone, Mrs. James W. Dean, Miss Margaret Lardner, Mrs. Andrew Loughlin, Miss Olga Morosoff, and Mrs. Lorenzo E. Pando for their able clerical assistance.

CONTENTS

THE VANISHING
RIGHT TO LIVE

THE PROBLEM

On April 28, 1967, a twenty-five-year-old professional boxer refused to step forward and be inducted into the armed forces of the United States of America:

> "It is in the light of my conscientiousness as a Muslim minister and on my own personal convictions that I take my stand in rejecting the call to be inducted in the armed services."

For this refusal to serve, Cassius Clay was stripped of his world heavyweight championship and subsequently was convicted and sentenced by a federal court to serve five years in prison and pay a $10,000 fine.

Three days earlier, Governor John A. Love of Colorado signed a law permitting so-called therapeutic abortion when a child is likely to be born with a grave and permanent physical or mental handicap; when pregnancy is the result of rape or incest; or when the pregnant woman would suffer permanent physical or mental harm by bearing a child.[1] The new law made Colorado the first state in the nation to permit abortion on these grounds.

On April 15, 1967, Black Power leader Stokely Carmichael urged his supporters at a "peace" demonstration in New York City to refuse to serve in the armed forces and led the thousands of listeners in chanting, "Hell, no, we ain't going." The April 15 rally, in the Sheep Meadow of New York's Central Park, featured a widely publicized burning of the American flag. This and similar incidents ultimately prompted Congress to pass a law forbidding such defilement of the flag. A few months before the flag burning, incidentally, Carmichael had been cheered wildly by 14,000 students, mostly white, at the University of California at Berkeley when he said, "To hell with the draft," and told them that the only way to stop the war in Vietnam was to refuse to cooperate with the draft.

The Vanishing Right to Live

What do draft evaders and abortion mills have in common? On the surface, not very much. However, if we penetrate beneath we find a common element—the notion of *non serviam*, I will not serve. The refusal to serve in the defense of one's country and the refusal to bear one's child involve a common refusal to serve others. We don't often think of abortion that way. But the refusal to serve is implicit there as it is in the evasion of the draft. Similarly, the refusal to assume another's burden, or even your own, is apparent in the unrestrained practice of birth control, in the advocacy of involuntary euthanasia to put elderly or other "useless" persons out of their misery (for their own good, of course), and in the involuntary sterilization of defectives to prevent them from generating offspring who would burden the rest of us.

In other ways as well, the flight from responsibility for others is a characteristic of our day. While Kitty Genovese was being stabbed to death outside her home in Kew Gardens, New York, at 3 A.M. on a March morning in 1964, thirty-eight of her neighbors heard her screams, opened their windows, saw what was happening—and went back to bed. Her battle with her slayer lasted more than half an hour and covered a distance of a hundred and fifty feet. Her assailant stabbed her and retreated, stabbed her and retreated, and finally came back and killed her. No one came to her aid. No one even called the police until a quarter of an hour after it was all over. The police arrived in two minutes, but it was too late. The affair precipitated a torrent of analyses and soul searching in the public print. Similar examples could be cited on a less dramatic scale. But the thirty-eight who watched Kitty Genovese die did more than betray their indifference. They epitomized a growing tendency of their day. As one college student in the neighborhood said a year later, "We are still apathetic slobs. People fend for themselves."[2]

The denial of responsibility for others is one side of the coin. The other is the flight from accountability for one's own actions. This is fairly obvious in abortion, unrestrained contraception, voluntary sterilization, and suicide. Similarly, draft evasion is a shirking of the responsibilities of citizenship. Of course, this is not to disparage the good faith of pacifists who sincerely refuse the call for reasons of conscience. We might well include Cassius Clay in this category. However, we need not accord the presumption of good

2

faith to those who, in preaching their peculiar brand of pacifism, weep only for the enemy and lose no opportunity to disparage their country.

The flight from responsibility for others and for our own acts can be seen in the soaring crime rate. Since 1960 serious crime has increased at a rate almost nine times the growth of the nation's population. Shoplifting, for instance, is now the fastest-growing form of theft in the country. Arrests for shoplifting have soared by 79% in the last five years. Recently a national drugstore chain gave lie detector tests to its employees and found that 74% of the workers had stolen goods from the firm. Each year thefts from stores by shoplifters and dishonest employees amount to 2 billion dollars, that is, ten dollars for each man, woman, child, and infant in the United States. In a typical comment, a security officer of a Houston store blamed the increasing thefts on "a gradual moral breakdown and lack of respect for others."

The Supreme Court of the United States has played a significant role in insulating criminals from the consequences of their acts, thereby contributing to the breakdown of personal responsibility. In a series of eccentric interpretations, the rights of criminal defendants have been inflated to the point where the state is increasingly unable to perform its basic duty of protecting the lives and property of its citizens. Convicted defendants seem to be implicitly presumed by the Court majority to be the victims of official oppression. Strained legalisms are too often used with the effect of exonerating the criminal from the penalty for his crime. The police and prosecutors are required to abide by elaborate and delicate rules ordained by the courts in such a way that the fair enforcement of the law is unrealistically impeded. The concentration on artificial distinctions has wholly obscured in many cases the issue of guilt or innocence. As Justice Benjamin Cardozo protested forty years ago, "The criminal is to go free because the constable has blundered."[3]

It is important to safeguard the procedural rights of the accused. At times the maintenance of those rights will necessarily result in the insulation of the guilty from punishment. And such freeing of the guilty is an inescapable incident of our protection of rights that must remain available to innocent and guilty alike. For it must be remembered that under our system an accused person is innocent until proven guilty beyond a reasonable doubt. But in implementing the constitutional protections a reasoned balance is to be sought. The courts exist not merely to shield the guilty but to enforce the law with even-handed impartiality as well. In the field of criminal law it should be remembered that the people, too, have rights. Unfortunately, today, the rights of the law-abiding majority are too often subordinated. It would be well for the Supreme Court to heed the admonition of the late Judge Learned Hand, of the United States Court of Appeals: "Our dangers do not lie in too little tenderness to the accused. Our procedure has been always haunted by the ghost of the innocent man convicted. It is an unreal dream. What we need to fear is the archaic formalism and the watery sentiment that obstructs, delays, and defeats the prosecution of crime."[4]

A related symptom of the decline of personal accountability is evidenced in the trend away from capital punishment. Capital punishment for crime is rare today, with only one execution in the United States in 1966 and two in 1967. I do not argue that the death penalty is necessarily a good thing. Rather, it is merely worth noting here that its abolition is frequently urged for the wrong reason. It is possible to argue that the supreme penalty does not sufficiently deter, that a concentration upon its preservation distracts attention from the urgent need for improving the basic criminal process, and that the end sought by capital punishment could be attained by a tightening of criminal procedures generally and a more realistic interpretation of constitutional protections. Unfortunately, however, the opposition to the death penalty is sometimes based upon the theory that the individual is not truly responsible for his actions and that therefore he ought not to pay an irreversible penalty for them. Society is said to be the culprit rather than the individual criminal. Or poverty is blamed, or some cause other than the personal decision of the malefactor.

The widespread campaign of "civil disobedience" illustrates again the trend toward irresponsibility. The pernicious doctrine of selective obedience to law denies that citizenship entails a general duty of obedience for the performance of which the state can properly hold the citizen accountable. Nor is the irresponsibility of this doctrine mitigated by the willingness of its proponents to accept penalties for their violation of law. They claim a moral sanction for their disobedience. While there are situations in which one may be morally justified and even required to disobey an unjust law, the contemporary deacons of discontent claim the right to violate even admittedly just laws, such as those against blocking traffic, as a means of protest against conditions to which they object. They exalt their personal judgments over the needs of the community and they scorn even to try the means available within the law for redressing their grievances. They threaten the Congress of the United States that unless their impossible demands are promptly met they will escalate their demonstrations to the point where chaos and violence will predictably result. This is a tactic wholly inimical to the legislative process in a representative government. Sanctimoniously, the Pied Pipers of discord lay claim to the moral approbation of the community. And too often they get it. Rather the preachers of organized civic irresponsibility should be visited with public contempt as well as with the full penalties of the law for their criminal conduct. For there is no such thing as "civil" disobedience. Rather it is disobedience of criminal laws and therefore criminal disobedience.

The breakdown of personal responsibility is evident also in the divorce rate, which shows that one out of every three marriages ends in divorce. After all, what is divorce but a flight from one's responsibility for another and a flight from accountability for one's solemnly undertaken contractual obligation?

More basically, perhaps, the prevailing welfare state and its supporting mentality prove that personal responsibility is a virtue honored in oratory but too widely disregarded in practice. This is not a brief for Herbert Spencer's social statics. Nor is it to deny or disparage the proper function of government to provide assistance to those who need it. But things have gone too far in this respect. The American of today is unloading onto the state an increasing share of his responsibility for himself and for others. Historian Barbara Tuchman rightly observed: "The welfare state has brought a transformation from the independent to the nurtured and supported society."[5] Back in 1960 the Roman Catholic bishops of the United States voiced their concern over this accelerating tendency. "The pressures are growing," the prelates wrote, "for a constantly greater reliance on the collectivity rather than the individual. An inordinate demand for benefits, most easily secured by the pressures of organization, has led an ever-growing number of our people to relinquish their rights and to abdicate their responsibilities."[6]

The survival of an orderly, free society requires a reversal of the manifold trend toward personal irresponsibility. But this reversal depends upon an awakening by each person to the fact that he is, under God, responsible for his own acts and responsible in a large way for others. The need is essentially one of the spirit. It is forlorn to hope, however, that the needed reform can be generated by piously preaching the platitudes of duty and responsibility. Rather, we need something more specific.

We could prompt a general renewal of responsibility by effecting a principled change in the public attitude toward certain basic and specific issues. There are many issues that are appropriate for this purpose, including the right of "civil" disobedience, the duty to serve in the armed forces, the broad area of criminal justice, and others. However, it will be useful to focus instead on other issues, which raise the question of responsibility but which directly and essentially involve another factor of primary importance—the right to live. Capital punishment, abortion, euthanasia, and suicide are suitable topics for use in this way to prompt an awakening of responsibility. These issues engage the public attitude and policy toward life itself. More precisely, they relate on the one hand to the extent to which innocent life will be protected, and, on the other, to the forfeitability of life, for example, through one's own criminal aggression. Other topics, including contraception, sterilization, homosexuality, and artificial insemination, do not involve the termination of life but rather its beginning. It is impossible, however, to generate a reverence for life without a due respect for its origins. And we can hardly expect a sound public regard for the right to life without promoting a coherent attitude toward the generative process and its relation to life itself. In each of these matters—artificial insemination, abortion, euthanasia, suicide, capital punishment, contraception, sterilization, and homosexuality—there is an interplay of personal responsibility for others and accountability for one's own acts. But there is also a common element of life and death. They directly involve the right to life itself, and if the people cannot be persuaded to assume their responsibilities on these issues it is unlikely that they will assume them on any other.

6

The Problem

Since Moses came down from Mount Sinai, the right to life has been affirmed in Judaic and Christian civilizations. Even before the Ten Commandments were issued, and even for those who, then or now, deny their authority, respect for innocent life has been mandated by the natural law, which was forcefully described by Sir Edward Coke:

> The Law of Nature is that which God at the time of Creation of the nature of man infused into his heart for his preservation and direction; and this is the eternal law, the moral law, called also the Law of Nature. And by this law, written with the finger of God in the heart of man, were the people of God a long time governed, before the law was written by Moses, who was the first reporter or writer of law in the world.[7]

The Declaration of Independence was based upon "the Laws of Nature and of Nature's God," and affirmed the basic character of the right to life:

> We hold these truths to be self-evident, that all men are created equal, that they are endowed by their Creator with certain unalienable Rights, that among these are Life, Liberty and the pursuit of Happiness.

The right to life, in Blackstone's phrase, is "a right inherent by nature in every individual." However, neither the right nor the command, "Thou shalt not kill," is absolute. The aggressor forfeits his right to life, according to the rule of self-defense, when he makes a deadly attack upon another. Similarly, the concept of a just war of defense implies that an aggressor nation forfeits the right to life of its soldiers and, in some cases, of its non-combatant civilians. The criminal's right to life has been commonly held, at least until recently, to yield before the state's power to inflict capital punishment. These and other refinements of "Thou shalt not kill" have been jealously limited, at least in principle.

Recently, however, contradictory interpretations of the right to life have been prominently advanced. Pacifists today, for example, emphasize the horror of war. They seem to imply that the citizen has no obligation to offer himself and his life in defense of the state when he disagrees with the political evaluations of those in authority. Also, some who preach resistance to the draft advocate permissive abortion as well. They deny the duty to risk one's life to preserve the nation. But they subject the innocent child in the womb to certain death, not to save lives or the state itself, but merely to

7

enhance the convenience and comfort of others. They would impose upon the child in the womb a duty to serve these lesser concerns when they would not impose a duty upon the fully grown citizen to come to the defense of society and the state. When the child in the womb is likely to be born defective, they would impose upon him a duty to die lest he be a burden on the state or on others. On the contrary, we who oppose abortion and support the draft proceed from a principle that consistently would protect innocent life against attack and yet would impose on the mature citizen a civic duty to serve unless exempted pursuant to law as a conscientious objector or otherwise. These supporters of abortion, however, would allow adults to evade their civic duty of military service and yet would require the unborn infant to sacrifice his life in furtherance of the similar evasion of duty by another which is so essential a feature of the usual abortion.

To kill defective children in the womb, of course, is no different in principle from the Nazi "final solution to the Jewish problem." But this does not seem to bother the liberal proponents of the scheme. The logical extension of abortion for this purpose is infanticide, the killing of unwanted children after they are born. Indeed, infanticide is more merciful, for at least it has the virtue of certainty and involves no danger to the life of the mother. When you abort a child who is likely to be born defective, you run a risk that you will abort a child who in fact would have turned out to be physically sound. It would be more scientific to wait until after the birth to see whether the child in fact is defective.

The notion that a newborn but unwanted infant should be slain at birth does not sit well with modern sensibilities. Although infanticide has few adherents today, the same remedy on the other end of the scale is widely proposed. Euthanasia is frequently advanced as an act of mercy. The innocent victim is to be killed "for his own good." But is it not really advocated, at least in enough cases to taint the whole practice, merely to save the killer or society from inconvenience? If so, it is a selfish denial of all responsibility to one's neighbor. A society in which involuntary euthanasia has a place would be a dehumanized society built upon counsels of despair. The sanctity of innocent life is similarly compromised by so-called voluntary euthanasia, which is a fancy term for permissive suicide. There is, of course, no obligation on an ill person or his relatives or doctors to take extraordinary means to preserve his life. However, it can only cheapen the value of life to give the irrevocable effect of a death warrant to the unnatural and inherently unreliable request to die of a patient who is either saturated with drugs or tormented by pain.

We need a stiffening of attitude on these and other issues of life. Hopefully, we can trigger a general reawakening of personal responsibility. The need for this is apparent also from the explosion of contraception as a nearly universal practice. Contraception differs from abortion in that contraception prevents a life from coming into existence, whereas abortion destroys one after it has begun. This book will not engage in a theological debate on the subject. Rather, we are concerned here because unrestrained contraception involves an assumption of sexual rights without accepting at least the possibility of the attendant responsibilities of parenthood. The unrestrained and deliberate practice of contraception does more than reduce the sexual act to an exercise of self-gratification rather than of love. It crystallizes the basic issues with which we are concerned, involving as it does a flight from accountability for one's own acts and a refusal to accept responsibility for others.

Although the prevention of life is different from the taking of existing life, the general attitude of a society toward contraception can measure the prevailing climate on the right to life in general. Subject to the question of means (that is, mechanical contraception, the pill, rhythm, etc.), all will agree that some type of family planning is legitimate in some circumstances. A society that regards family planning as a necessary evil may still be said to have a reverential attitude toward human life. On the other hand, a society that views contraception as an inalienable right under any and all circumstances betrays a certain irresponsibility toward life. It is not surprising that many who advocate unrestrained contraception or the use of coercive contraception as an instrument of state population policy will be found also to favor permissive abortion and euthanasia. For one common element in these positions is a disparagement of the right to live. The issues join in another way when it is remembered that some contraceptive agents are themselves abortifacients.

Sterilization is a form of contraception. There are several types of sterilization to be considered. Involuntary sterilization as a punishment for crime is probably irrelevant to the prevention of crime. Involuntary sterilization for eugenic purposes is reminiscent of Nazi Germany in its primitive violation of basic rights. However, voluntary sterilization is the type most prominently at issue today. This is a form of contraception, distinguished from other forms by its permanence. But it raises the same issues as the more orthodox contraceptive techniques. While a person who uses a contraceptive device can say that he admits the possibility of participating in the act of creation at some future time, one who procures his own sterilization has no such defense. No one would seek to be sterilized unless the sexual act meant a great deal to him. But in exchange for what he hopes will be a lifetime of uninhibited enjoyment of the thing most important to him, he has in fact condemned himself to a life of irresponsible sexual adolescence and he has deprived that very act of its intrinsic meaning. That meaning cannot endure if we have willfully prevented even the possibility of cooperation in the creation of a new life.

This book will argue for a firmer attitude and policy toward these and other related issues. However, it will not advance any concept that the right to life is absolute. Rather, a sound analysis should view the right to life in relation to the broader concept of due process of law. Basically, the right to life means the right to be secure in the enjoyment of one's life and to forfeit it only in accordance with the dictates of valid law. And valid law in this connection means not merely a law enacted pursuant to prescribed procedures, but also a law in accord with elementary canons of fairness and the nature of man. Due process addresses itself to substance as well as procedure. Procedurally, it ensures notice and an opportunity for a fair hearing. Substantively, it protects against enactments that infringe upon a basic right or are, in their content, arbitrary, capricious, or unreasonable.

The insulation of the right to life from arbitrary abridgement is well founded in Western tradition and Anglo-Saxon law. When the barons exacted the pledges of the Magna Carta from King John at Runnymede in 1215, they included the promise that "No free man shall be taken or imprisoned or dispossessed, or outlawed, or banished, or in any way destroyed, nor will we go upon him, nor send upon him, except by the legal judgment of his peers or by the law of the land." In 1628, the Petition of Right affirmed "That no man of what estate or condition that he be, should be put out of his land or tenements, nor taken, nor imprisoned, nor disherited, nor put to death without being brought to answer by due process of law."

This principle, that the right to life may be invaded only pursuant to due process of law, found its way into a number of charters and proclamations in the American colonies. The Declaration and Resolves of the First Continental Congress in 1774 proclaims that the inhabitants of the colonies "are entitled to life, liberty and property: and they have never ceded to any foreign power whatever, a right to dispose of either without their consent."[8] The Declaration of Independence reiterated the pre-eminence of the right to live.

A more comprehensive proclamation of the right to live is found in the Declaration of Rights of the state of Delaware, adopted on September 11, 1776:

> That every member of society hath a right to be protected in the enjoyment of life, liberty and property, and therefore is bound to contribute his proportion towards the expense of that protection, and yield his personal service when necessary, or an equivalent thereto; but no part of a man's property can be justly taken from him or applied to public uses without his consent or that of his legal Representatives: Nor can any man that is conscientiously scrupulous of bearing arms in any case be justly compelled thereto if he will pay such equivalent.[9]

It is interesting to note that this Delaware declaration asserts not only the right to life but also the obligations incumbent upon the citizen from its possession.

Other state constitutions reaffirmed the immunity of the right to life from any invasion except according to due process of law. The Bill of Rights, adopted as the first ten amendments to the United States Constitution in 1791, incorporated this concept into our fundamental written law. The Fifth Amendment provides that no person shall be "deprived of life, liberty, or property, without due process of law." The Fourteenth Amendment, adopted in 1868, provides a similar protection against infringement by state governments.

The right to live is crucial. In some areas, such as abortion and euthanasia, we seek to preserve life from termination except in accord with due process of law. In other matters, such as sterilization, we seek to reinforce the right to life by cultivating an active reverence for it and for the God-given capacity through which we share in its creation. In all respects, a renewed reverence for life will increase our sense of personal responsibility to ourselves, to others, and to our Creator.

A special sense of urgency is imparted to this effort by the growing power of science to manipulate the origin and physical character of persons. Scientists now have the power to engage in selective breeding through artificial insemination. Other discoveries make possible the manipulation of genetic codes to produce desired changes in offspring. The technique of mass contraception by inoculation or by treating food and water supplies will be a reality in the very near future. Antidotes will be available to those who desire them or, in a regimented state, to those who are deemed worthy. And compulsory abortion will always be available to take care of the accidental pregnancies of those who are considered unfit to reproduce.

The implications are obvious, and enormous. The state will be able to deny the very power of generation to all except the favored class or race. And through compulsory artificial insemination the state will be able to produce tailor-made human beings from those who are allowed to procreate. At the other end of life, the theory of euthanasia has regathered its strength after the setback it suffered when Hitler applied it for all the world to see. The essence of the theory is that there are lives not worth living and that there are disposable people. As Professor Ian Donald of Glasgow University said, "We are on the slippery slope to having disposable citizens, because they are too ill or infirm to be socially or politically useful. Beware of those all too ready to usurp the functions and responsibilities of a god and start suggesting who shall be born, and who not, who shall live and which die."[10]

In approaching these matters, let us keep in mind our primary goal. It is to reawaken responsibility for others and accountability for one's own acts. These qualities, so necessary to a free and orderly society, are markedly in eclipse today. Eight general areas, directly involving life itself, will be used to illustrate the decline of these attributes today. While each of the chapters, with slight modification, could stand as a separate essay, they are arranged here with an eye to their interrelation and with a definite sequence in mind. The little known technique of artificial insemination is chosen to lead off because it shows the extent to which science has endowed man with the capacity to manipulate life itself. The potential uses of artificial insemination evoke an image of 1984. And our inclination is to wonder what sort of thinking could lead us to countenance those uses even in theory. But the answer is to be found in other areas, where ostensibly humanitarian reforms provide an entry for principles inevitably destructive of that reverence for life without which we cannot survive in freedom. Abortion reform, for example, is advanced as a humane effort to harmonize our law with both medical science and compassion for an afflicted mother. However, in fact it disregards the rights of the innocent victim, it ratifies the principle that life itself can be manipulated and even destroyed to advance the selfish concerns of others, and it hardens us to accept further inroads on that right. Abortion, therefore, is appropriate as a second chapter. Next, euthanasia will be treated, because it is a logical extension of the abortion principles and because it introduces the question of the power to procure one's own death voluntarily. This latter aspect leads us into our next topic, which is suicide. Here we confront the question of whether an adult, in full possession of his faculties, can voluntarily kill himself. Our conclusion here will ultimately depend upon our acknowledgment of a Creator to Whom life itself is owed. And one's attitude toward suicide will be indicative of one's respect for life on the other issues involved. There is one case, however, in which respect for innocent life can require the taking of life. When an aggressor takes the life of an innocent victim he can be held to forfeit his own, not for vengeance's sake, but as a security for the lives of innocent potential victims of himself or other criminals. And capital punishment raises starkly the issue of personal accountability for one's own acts.

We shall next consider contraception. Where abortion, euthanasia, suicide, and capital punishment relate to the destruction of life, contraception prevents a life from ever existing. Unlike artificial insemination, it is not a manipulation. Rather, to the extent it is practiced, it is a total frustration. It is useful to contrast it to those issues that involve the destruction or manipulation of life and yet to point out the basic irresponsibility common to all of them. Similarly, sterilization, which will be the following chapter, raises the same issues with the added note that it involves a permanent change of status and a consequently greater irresponsibility. Finally, the chapter on homosexuality is necessary because its recent increase is a phenomenon closely allied to the prevailing flight from responsibility. There is no intention here to disparage those who may be ensnared by homosexual tendencies beyond their control. Nevertheless, when we derogate the right to live by subordinating it to lesser and selfish concerns, as we see in abortion, unrestrained contraception, and other practices, it is not surprising that our tolerance of the unnatural increases. For when a mother kills the child committed to her most intimate protection and when unrestrained contraception wholly exalts the transiently pleasurable over the creative, nature is wronged as fully as by the union of persons of the same sex. Perhaps the element of irresponsibility is more evident in the homosexual area. But it is no different in kind from that which we find in the others. And the practice of homosexuality does symbolize in a special way the disdain for the origins of life with which we are concerned.

This book, then, is an appeal for a renewed reverence for life. This is an end worthy in itself of our utmost attention. But its attainment will serve to enkindle anew the flame of duty and responsibility. "No man is an island," said John Donne. We are responsible for others in a peculiarly human way, but if we are to acquit ourselves of this duty, we must first be answerable for our actions to ourselves and to God.

The total state is in the offing, endowed by the god of science with the power to rival the God of Creation. While there is yet time, those who believe in God and in the sanctity of the life He creates and sustains must deny to the secular state the power to violate that life. Only if the people assume their responsibility to promote respect for life and to insist upon its observance can the free society endure. For the untrammeled power of life and death is of the essence of tyranny. And the denial of that power to the state is the first condition of liberty.

2

ARTIFICIAL INSEMINATION

To have children was the dream of Stanley and Annette Gursky. Unfortunately, Mr. Gursky was impotent. Acting on a doctor's advice, they agreed that Mrs. Gursky should be artificially inseminated with the semen of an unknown third-party donor. As a result, Minday Frances Gursky was born on September 14, 1961. On her birth certificate, Annette Gursky was listed as the mother, which she was, and Stanley as the father, which he was not. Later, unfortunately, the marriage went on the rocks and the Gurskys became antagonists in court. In 1963, Justice Mark A. Costantino of the New York State Supreme Court in Kings County held that Minday was not Mr. Gursky's legitimate child.[1] Mr. Gursky had not formally adopted the child as his own, and the court ruled that his acquiescence in the artificial insemination procedure could not confer legitimacy on the child. In the view of the court, Minday was born out of wedlock, by a father other than the mother's husband. Indeed, the court indicated that it regarded the mother's submission to the insemination as adultery. However, the court decided that Mr. Gursky's consent to the process made him liable to support the child, even though she was illegitimate. More recently, however, a California court held that such a husband could not be convicted of a crime under a statute making it a criminal offense for a father to refuse to support his legitimate or illegitimate child.[2] Mr. Gursky had not been prosecuted for a crime, but had merely been required to support the child.[3]

Artificial insemination is of two types, one (homologous) when the seminal fluid of a husband is injected by mechanical means into his wife so as to induce conception, and the other (heterologous) when the seed is that of a "donor" other than the husband. For convenience, we shall refer to the former as AIH, to the latter as

15

AID, and to artificial insemination in general as AI. The first recorded AIH was performed in England in 1799. The first successful AIH in the United States was accomplished in 1866 by Dr. J. Marion Sims, of South Carolina, who later abandoned the technique as immoral. In the United States, AID appears to have been practiced first in the 1890s.

For many childless couples who want children, adoption is not wholly satisfactory, principally because of the long delays.[4] Others object to adoption because of the lack of fulfillment of the maternal urge and the absence of the inheritable characteristics of either spouse in the adopted child.[5] Artificial insemination, both AIH and AID, can be performed with a high degree of mechanical success and no unusual danger of infection or miscarriage. It has been estimated that there are between 5000 and 10,000 cases of AID in the United States each year, 3000 per year in England, and 1000 per year each in France and Germany.[6] The United States leads all countries in AID and Israel is second.[7] There are up to 150,000 living Americans who have been conceived by AID.[8] It must be remembered, though, that statistics are even less useful here than elsewhere, owing to the normal atmosphere of secrecy enshrouding an artificial insemination, and to the deliberate falsification of records encouraged by it. Although it is difficult to gauge with accuracy the extent of artificial insemination, the conclusion may safely be drawn that "it has certainly increased enormously" in recent years, both in this country and in England.[9]

AIH is free from virtually all legal difficulties. AID, on the other hand, is a wellspring of legal problems, real and imaginary. They include the issues of adultery, legitimacy, and the liability of the husband to support the child. Of secondary importance are such matters as the liability of the inseminating doctor and the donor, the customary falsification of birth records, and possible subsequent intermarriage of related offspring of the same donor.

The problem of adultery has been the most productive of litigation concerning AID. In 1921 the Ontario Supreme Court labeled AID as "a monstrous act of adultery," since it involved "the voluntary surrender to another person of the . . . reproductive powers or faculties of the guilty person."[10] In the court's view, the essence of adultery lies not in any "moral turpitude" or physical act, but rather in the fact that "in the case of the woman, it involves the possibility of introducing into the family of the husband a false strain of blood."

The question of adultery has not been definitively settled in the United States. And there have been few cases on the point. For example, in 1945, an Illinois court ventured the opinion that AID is not adultery.[11] Later, a New York court noted in passing that a child born by AID is as legitimate as "a child born out of wedlock who by law is made legitimate upon the marriage of the interested parties."[12] The court's equation of an AID child with one "born out of wedlock" implicitly acknowledges that an AID impregnation is extramarital in nature. If the court's analogy is correct, it is difficult to see why the wife's submission to AID is not adultery, in some non-technical sense of the term. In 1954, Judge Gorman of the Superior Court of Cook County, Illinois, declared that, while AIH is wholly unobjectionable in law, AID is contrary to public policy, is adultery on the part of the wife, and a child so conceived is illegitimate.[13] As an illegitimate, the court said, the child is the mother's alone, and the husband can have no interest in the child. An appeal was dismissed by the appellate court[14] without discussion of the question of AI.

The commission appointed by the Archbishop of Canterbury in its report on the subject[15] stated, "It seems to us that adultery involves the surrender of the reproductive powers or the organs of generation, whether capable of actual generation or not." However, any attempt to fit AID into the precast mold of adultery is bound to involve contradictions and absurdities. For example, if the donor has died before the wife is impregnated with his seed (such can happen where a "sperm bank" is used), the wife would be in the anomalous situation of committing adultery with a dead man. A far better approach would be to by-pass the concept of adultery and to treat AID as what it is, a new problem.

There are other theoretically perplexing problems collateral to the main issues of adultery and illegitimacy. For example, what can be done to, or for, the doctor who conducts the insemination? Would he be liable for malpractice if he were negligent? It is hard to see why he should not be. Would he be liable for breach of warranty if the sperm were of inferior quality? Not only would this be difficult to prove, but one can envision disputes about the genetic "quality" of sperm that would do credit to a debate at a livestock breeders' convention. Where the AID is performed without the husband's consent, the doctor conceivably could be liable for interfering with family relations and the wife could possibly be guilty of a fraud upon her husband. The procurement by the doctor of releases from the parties would not necessarily protect him against criminal prosecution and might not be of much assistance to him in defending a civil action.[16] Finally, although this list is by no means exhaustive of theoretical bases of liability, the doctor could be guilty of fraud or forgery for knowingly registering the husband on the birth certificate as the father of the AID child. This possibility is of real significance, and such falsification presents a genuine threat to the reliability of public records.[17] Some doctors have adopted the practice of referring the case, after insemination, to another physician for actual delivery of the baby; the second physician, unaware of the AID, registers the husband as the father with no conscious falsification. This practice, however, does not eliminate the fraud, but rather perpetrates it through the pen of an innocent agent.

One result of this falsification of records, and of the general secrecy enveloping AID, could be unwitting intermarriage between offspring of the same donor. This likelihood has been discounted and ignored by some advocates of AID, but it is an inevitably practical problem. Multiple donations by a single donor are quite common. We know of at least one donor whose talents for vicarious generation were successfully exerted upon thirty-five women.[18] The frequency of donations may be accounted for, at least in part, by the zeal of medical students, who are a frequent source of supply, and by the more prosaic fact that donors are generally paid. In any event, it is not entirely fanciful to envision intermarriage by children of the same donor.

Conceivably, the donor could be held to an obligation to support his offspring. This would appear to be a desirable result in principle, and would tend to reduce the broadcast procreation that can lead to incest and a general disregard for personal responsibilities. In fact, the greatest deterrent to the practice of AID would be to make donors of sperm liable to support their test-tube offspring and to enable the offspring to inherit from the donor. But if the donor supports the child, would he not be entitled to custody of the child or at least to visitation rights? A donor could plausibly argue that his contribution to the child's very existence entitles him to something more than the privilege of paying his bills. Also, if the donor were to make a knowingly or negligently false representation to the doctor about his background and characteristics, he could possibly be liable for the damage caused by his unrevealed defects. In a different vein, there is the possibility that an unscrupulous donor who learned the identities of the recipients of his favor might resort to blackmail; conversely, a donor could be a likely target himself for blackmail.

Only a few statutes have been enacted to regulate the practice of artificial insemination. Article 21 of the Health Code of the City of New York prescribes certain medical tests for the donor and would-be mother, requires the keeping of records, and by implication regulates the "sperm banks" where stored sperm is kept. This ordinance conveys a tacit approval of AID, but the approval is less emphatic in light of the provocation that led to its adoption. In 1947 a number of physicians in New York City received this notice from an enterprising individual with a Bachelor of Science degree:

> We offer semen drawn from healthy and investigated professional donors. Suitable types for your patients' specifications. Active specimens guaranteed and delivered daily. Confidential service—office hours 5:30 to 7 P.M.

There followed the name and address of the proprietor. The Sanitary Code provision was adopted as a reaction to this unique venture in free enterprise.

In 1967, Oklahoma became the first, and so far the only, state in the Union to make a child conceived by AID the legitimate child of the husband and wife who consented to the procedure.[19] Supporters of the law called it "the first progressive piece of legislation in a long time." "Where can you say it is morally wrong for a woman who could not have a baby to now have one?" asked one lawmaker. "This bill is a godsend," he concluded, with a small g. Another, however, said, "I don't think people should be treated as cattle. This is putting the human being on the same level as four-legged animals. It won't make for good relations between husbands and wives. I think this is morally wrong and goes against the teachings of the Bible."[20]

AID can obviously have a great effect, for good or ill, on the family unit. An emphatic approval of AID is offered by one doctor in these words:

> Only occasionally do problems arise in the home where a baby has been born of artificial insemination; the results are, in the main, excellent. The wife has given birth to her child, thus satisfying her maternal instinct; the husband has "fathered" a child and in the eyes of the world his virility has been established; the child experiences even more love than the ordinary child, since he had been sought eagerly and with much effort. In fact, all three members of the family comprise a happy home. The proof of such a state of contentment is evidenced by the fact that a large percentage of the couples return for a second baby to be conceived by this method.[21]

Another argues that illustrations from other societies "indicate that it is possible for a society's family organization to operate in a stable fashion with the reproductive function partly outside."[22] Advocates of AID emphasize the blessings brought to the barren family by the AID child. Unfortunately, their rhetoric tends at times to extravagance. For instance, Dr. Joseph Fletcher mentions a physician in England who had been artificially inseminating unmarried women on the ground that "it is every woman's heritage to bear a child . . . artificial insemination provides the unmarried business woman with a decent and moral method of acquiring the children nature intended her to bear."[23] Perhaps we can take refuge in the immortal lines of Edgar Smith, as sung by Marie Dressler in *Tillie's Nightmare:*

> "You may tempt the upper classes
> With your villainous demi-tasses,
> But Heaven will protect the Working Girl."

Opponents of AID strongly deny that AID can be the bond to cement a family into an enduring unit. As one doctor put it:

> It has been said . . . that one reason why certain married couples seek artificial insemination is to conceal infertility. This indicates immediately that they are already experiencing difficulties in meeting and successfully coping with the realities of life. If they cannot face and accept certain physical inadequacies, how can they expect to meet the additional problems presented by parenthood which presupposes that the individual is expected to have developed full emotional maturity? It suggests that they are avoiding reality and this neuropathic trait is so frequently associated with the psychoneurotic, the pre-psychotic and the psychotic person. What chance would

the resultant child have of obtaining full emotional maturity himself in a basically unstable environment?[24]

To the same effect is this statement by Dr. Ruth W. Berenda, a psychoanalyst and formerly a member of the Psychiatric Clinic of New York City's Domestic Relations Court:

When a couple adopt a child, they admit openly that they cannot have one of their own. But when they are the parents of an artificially inseminated child they often conceal the true facts and try to present a front of normality. The result—both a self-deception and a deception to the world—can be harmful to their relationship. . . . And I am not at all certain that most stable men would be willing to act as donors.[25]

In 1957 the practice of AID was "entirely suspended in New South Wales, Victoria and Queensland, because of family breakdowns and the grave religious and legal problems created."[26] The degrading aspects of AID have led some to regard it frankly as a worse evil than divorce. As one critic said, "It is hardly in keeping with the dignity of the human race to treat a man as if he were a stallion at stud. . . . It is well arguable that, from a wider point of view, divorce with all its evils is preferable to the saving of a few marriages by this means."[27]

Religious opinion is sharply divided on the morality of AI. AIH has attracted disapproval only from the Catholic Church and from some spokesmen of the Church of England.[28] AID, on the other hand, has given rise to a wide variety of opinions. There are various positions among Protestant and Jewish theologians on the subject. Pope Pius XII, however, unequivocally condemned AID as well as AIH in 1949:

The husband and wife alone have a reciprocal right over their bodies in order to engender a new life; and this right is exclusive, untransferrable, inalienable. This ought to be so, too, from a consideration for the child. Nature imposes on the person who gives life to a baby the duty of its conservation and of its education, by very reason of the bond established. But no bond of origin, no moral and juridical bond of conjugal procreation, exists between the legitimate husband and the child who is the fruit of the active element of a third party—even in the case where the husband has given his consent.

In a later address, he reaffirmed this position:

The conjugal act in its natural structure . . . is much more than the mere union of two life-germs, which can be brought about also artificially, that is, without the natural act of the spouses. The conjugal act, as it is planned and willed by nature, implies a personal cooperation, the right to which the parties have mutually conferred on each other in contracting marriage.[29]

The most important practical aspect of AID today is its potential use for the production of tailor-made human beings. In 1967 two scientists at Stanford University announced that they had manufactured a synthetic DNA (deoxyribonucleic acid). DNA is the basic material that controls heredity. Arthur Kornberg, one of the discoverers, described it as the "closest thing yet to creating life in a laboratory," and he predicted that modification of genes to produce specific changes in human beings might be possible within a decade.[30] President Johnson, on congratulating the two biochemists, said their "awesome accomplishment" had "unlocked a fundamental secret of life." He said the announcement was one of "the most important news stories you ever read, or your daddy read or your granddaddy read."[31]

The manipulation of chromosomes and genes to produce desired changes in human offspring has enormous implications. However, a more direct means toward this end already exists in the technique of artificial insemination. It is clearly adaptable for eugenic ends. As one doctor enthused: "Who knows but that in this way we might even be able to prevent another Hitler or some similar aberration of the genes. Is this not one of the easiest and most direct ways of improving offspring and promoting a life of less personal heartbreak and of greater happiness for the entire human race?"[32]

Nobel Laureate Dr. Hermann Muller of the University of Indiana, who won the Nobel prize for discoveries in genetics, urges that this technique be used for that very purpose. Referring to artificial insemination, he claims, "The means exist right now of achieving a much greater, speedier, and more significant genetic improvement of the population by the use of selection, than could be effected by the most sophisticated methods of treatment of the genetic material that might be available in the twenty-first century. The obstacles to carrying out such an improvement by selection are psychological ones, based on antiquated traditions from which we can emancipate ourselves. . . ."

Dr. Muller would engineer his selective improvement of the

human race through the use of sperm banks from which the sperm of superior donors would be used to generate superior offspring:

> Its proposed mode of procedure is to establish banks of stored germ cells (spermatozoa), eventually ample banks, derived from persons of very diverse types, but including, as far as possible, those whose lives had given evidence of outstanding gifts of mind, merits of disposition and character, or physical fitness. From these germinal stores couples would have the privilege of selecting such material, for the engendering of children of their own families, as appeared to them to afford the greatest promise of endowing their children with the kind of heredity constitution that came nearest to their own ideals.[33]

The assumption underlying Dr. Muller's selective breeding program is that there are in fact criteria by which superior donors of sperm can be selected. Dr. Muller answers the lament of an earlier doctor who wrote:

> Physicians to the human race are, in comparison with physicians to dumb brutes, leagues behind in both scientific investigation and the successful practice of artificial insemination. To be sure, we are trammeled by conventions, moral codes and frailties of human character, which never hinder the stockbreeder.[34]

Dr. Alan Guttmacher, who uttered this plea, wrote that he would test the donor by asking himself: "Is that the kind of man whom I would like my daughter to marry?" One critic, however, was less enthusiastic:

> If I had a daughter, I would not want her to marry a man whose sense of moral values was such that he would calmly enter a doctor's office or laboratory and ejaculate his semen into a glass jar for a sum of money.[35]

One scientific difficulty with Dr. Muller's proposal is that the offspring of the artificial insemination might well be born with defects that were latent in the seemingly superior donor. But of course there are more fundamental implications. As Rabbi Immanuel Jakobovits said, "Such human stud-farming exposes society to the gravest dangers which can never be outweighed by the benefits that may accrue in individual cases."[36] Nevertheless, the Muller proposal is entirely within the power of science today.

Even now, frozen sperm can be kept alive and potent for months. It is reasonable to expect that, in the not too distant future, it will be possible to preserve sperm for years so that it can even be used in future generations. In the opposite direction, as we shall note in Chapter VII, we can foresee the development of chemical contraceptives that can be added to food and water supplies for mass consumption. This development would actualize the cheap and unsuspected technique for mass genocide so avidly sought by Heinrich Himmler and the other Nazi planners. An entire race or population could be wiped off the face of the earth and the exterminators would not have to forgo the use of the enforced labor of the current, and last, generation. Even more ominously, a tyrannical regime could use chemical contraceptives to liquidate a dissident population while using frozen sperm to build a master race.

Similarly, contraceptive vaccination is within the reach of science.[37] Those deemed unworthy to procreate could be sterilized by a simple injection. This prospect is reminiscent of Sir Julian Huxley, who urged that persons with low IQs or who were otherwise genetically subnormal should be prevented from reproducing. If they had offspring, they would interfere with the grand design of science. "It is up to us," said Sir Julian, "to plan a society which will favor the increase instead of the decrease of man's desirable genetic capacities for intelligence and imagination, empathy and cooperation, and a sense of discipline and duty."[38]

Science has given the modern state the tools with which to play God. At one end of the scale, the statists are reaching for the power to determine who shall die and when. Abortion and euthanasia, both reduced to an exact science, are examples of this power used to dispose of the inconvenient innocent. At the other end of the scale, contraception, sterilization, and artificial insemination offer the statists, for the first time in history, the chance to decide who shall be born and what physical characteristics they shall have. The eugenics engineers literally can play God. And they apparently have every intention of doing so. Artificial insemination, as outlined by Dr. Muller and others of similar mind, is a tool ready at hand for the purpose. It is not without significance that George Orwell's world of 1984 is one in which "All children were to be begotten by artificial insemination ("artsem," it was called in Newspeak) and brought up in public institutions."[39]

If we would curb the tendency to cheapen human life and to manipulate it in the interest of the state, we must curb the practice of artificial insemination. But there are several distinctions that have to be made in the process. AIH should not be regulated specifically by law. The social danger is minimal, and existing medical practice sufficiently safeguards the cleanliness and integrity of the procedure. However, the performance of AID, with or without the consent of the husband, should be made a criminal offense on the part of the doctor, or other implementing intermediary, and the donor. If AID were made criminal on the part of the mother and her husband, that could have a harmful effect in inhibiting adoptions in those cases where AID might be performed in violation of the law or in states not prohibiting AID. AID should not be declared to be adultery, but if performed without the husband's consent, it could possibly be sufficient cruelty to enable the husband to obtain a civil divorce under the laws of some states.

AID children should be declared by statute to be illegitimate, whether the AID was with or without the consent of the husband. This rule should have only prospective effect; the tangle that would result from a retrospective decree of the illegitimacy of the thousands of AID children, who are regarded as legitimate by their families and some courts, would be insoluble. A rule of illegitimacy would seem to be dictated by the inherently extramarital nature of AID, and would bar the possibility of an unwanted, or at most a tolerated, intrusion by an AID child into the husband's inheritance pattern. In most states an illegitimate child can inherit only from its mother. If the husband wishes to provide for the child, he can do so by will or he can adopt the child. The donor, however, should be required to support the child if no one else does and the child should be allowed to inherit from the donor. Although this rule, too, should have only prospective effect, it is very important. An imposition of financial responsibility on the donor is the key to a swift, painless abolition of AID.

Adoption procedures should be liberalized to permit greater secrecy and dispatch in the adoption of AID children. Even assuming the illegality of AID, there should be a mechanism for adopting AID children already born and those who may thereafter be born in violation of the law or in states not prohibiting AID. The falsification of birth records should be strictly prosecuted, with criminal sanctions imposed upon all parties knowingly participating in the fraud. A proper birth record entry should be made a prerequisite for adoption of the AID child by the husband. As a practical matter, nothing can be done about the false entries already made, with the possible exception of a privilege to correct past false entries without criminal liability. And if the corrected entries show a present husband and wife to be AID offspring of the same donor, we can only throw in the towel.

However, regardless of the difficulty of shaping a remedy here, something must be done to restrict the practice of artificial insemination. For, in principle, it threatens the stability of the family. And in practice it is too easily adaptable to the purposes of those who would claim for themselves the power to determine the character of future generations. Reproduction, rather, is a personal responsibility, under God. And it is essential to prevent the erosion of that responsibility. Artificial insemination may be the most striking manifestation of that erosion. But its popularity is merely a symptom of the basic irresponsibility involved in other matters, including particularly abortion.

3

ABORTION

> My mother did not want a seventh child, so she decided to get rid of me before I was born. Then a marvelous thing happened. My aunt dissuaded her, and so I was permitted to be born. Think of it! It was a miracle![1]

The speaker: Artur Rubinstein, by common assent "the world's greatest pianist." He was almost, by his mother's assent, dismembered by an abortionist's knife.

Nothing so dramatizes the low estate of the right to life as the wide acceptance of abortion. Abortion, as distinguished from an unintended miscarriage, is the intentional expulsion of the child from the womb before he is able to lead an independent existence. Its necessary and desired end is the death of the child. The present law in most states permits abortion only where necessary to preserve the life of the mother. Thus the life of the unborn child is immune from termination except as an inescapable incident to the preservation of the life of the mother.

In 1959 the American Law Institute included in its proposed Model Penal Code a provision that would allow abortion whenever a licensed physician "believes there is a substantial risk that continuance of the pregnancy would gravely impair the physical or mental health of the mother or that the child would be born with a grave physical or mental defect or that the pregnancy resulted from rape, incest or other felonious intercourse."[2] In 1967, Colorado,[3] North Carolina,[4] and California[5] became the first states to break the generally prevailing rule forbidding abortion except to save the life of the mother. These three states adopted new laws modeled substantially on the recommendation of the American Law Institute, except that the California legislature deleted the authorization of abortion where the child is likely to be deformed. Governor Ronald Reagan had protested that the provision was "only a step away from what

Hitler tried to do."[6] However, the drive to relax the abortion laws continues unabated. The law in Great Britain was recently amended to allow abortion on grounds similar to those recommended by the American Law Institute and also where the birth of the child would cause injury to the physical or mental health of any existing children of the mother's family.[7]

There are probably about 10,000 legal abortions in the United States every year and anywhere from 100,000 to 1,000,000 illegal abortions. It is virtually impossible to obtain any reliable statistics in the area of illegal abortions and it is likely that the actual figure is not even close to 1,000,000.[8] Moreover, the proponents of abortion "reform" concede that their proposals would legalize at most only about 20% of the abortions currently illegally performed.[9] Of course the issue is not the number of abortions, legal or illegal. Rather, in this matter of life and death, our concern should not depend upon the numbers of lives involved.

Nor can this be dismissed as a "religious" issue. Although Roman Catholics are most prominent among the opponents of abortion, their cause is not a merely Catholic preserve. Rabbi Immanuel Jakobovits, for example, is outspoken in his condemnation of abortion. Karl Barth, Paul Ramsey, and Dietrich Bonhoeffer are among the Protestant theologians opposed to abortion. Bonhoeffer writes, "To raise the question whether we are here concerned already with a human being or not is merely to confuse the issue. The simple fact is that God certainly intended to create a human being and that this nascent human being has been deliberately deprived of his life. And that is nothing but murder."[10] Of course many who oppose abortion do so primarily out of a religious conviction that abortion violates the law of God. Indeed that is the basic motive impelling the writing of this chapter. However, that motivation should not cause us to discount the compelling secular and constitutional reasons against abortion. It is much more satisfying to say simply that abortion violates the law of God, period. However, the case can also be made on secular and pragmatic grounds, and it is incumbent on the opponents of abortion to do so as well as to condemn it on account of the unyielding divine prohibition.

The critical issue here is whether the child in the womb is a human being and, particularly, whether he is such from the moment of conception. If he is, then one can hardly urge that he be killed to suit the convenience or comfort of others (even in the most poignant and aggravated cases where he was conceived in rape or incest) or because those others consider him unfit to live on account of some deformity or abnormality. More precisely, the critical issue is where to give the benefit of the doubt. Our civilization and law are premised on the belief that the benefit of the doubt should always be accorded to life rather than death. Thus we demand proof beyond all reasonable doubt before we execute a criminal or even subject him to fine or imprisonment. This benefit of the doubt should be given all the more freely to the child in the womb where there can be no doubt that, if he is alive at all, he is wholly innocent of any wrongful intent. Since the only issue is whether he is a living human being, the obvious absence of culpability on his part should impel us to resolve all doubts in favor of his survival.

It can be proven to the satisfaction of any impartial observer that human life actually begins at the moment of conception. However, we do not have to sustain this burden. Rather, those who support liberalized abortion can do so only if they can say that, beyond any and all reasonable doubt, human life does not begin at the moment of conception. If there is any doubt whatever, our tradition and civilization dictate the resolution of that doubt in favor of innocent life rather than death. There are some who disagree as to whether human life begins at conception. However, no supporter of abortion liberalization can say that, beyond any reasonable doubt, life does not begin at conception. Our obligation, therefore, is clearly to accord the benefit of the doubt to innocent life in this matter.

A few samples of the available scientific and legal opinion will indicate how unsound it is for anyone to claim that, beyond any doubt, life does not begin at conception. If the relevant authorities do not at least raise a doubt in favor of the child, then rational demonstration would appear to have become impossible. Actually, the authorities demonstrate beyond a reasonable doubt that life does in fact begin at conception.

The eminent embryologist, Dr. Bradley M. Patten of the University of Michigan Medical School, wrote in his basic text, *Human Embryology*, that the union of the male sperm and the female ovum "initiates the life of a new individual."[11] It begins "a new individual life history."[12] Thereafter, he wrote, the process of development is one of growth and "birth is but a convenient landmark in a continuous process."[13]

Dr. Floyd L. Ruch, in his standard college text, *Psychology and Life*, wrote in a similar vein that, "At the time of conception, two living germ cells—the sperm from the father and the egg, or ovum, from the mother—unite to produce a new individual."[14]

Another authority, Dr. Herbert Ratner, director of public health of Oak Park, Illinois, wrote:

> It is now of unquestionable certainty that a human being comes into existence precisely at the moment when the sperm combines with the egg. How do we know this? From everything we know about genetics. When the sperm and egg nuclei unite, all of the characteristics, such as the color of the eyes, hair, skin, that make a unique personality, are laid down determinatively. That's why a physician—even without any kind of formal ethical education, moral teaching or even philosophical sophistication—relying solely on medical science, knows, when he performs an abortion, that he is killing another human being. After all, the fetus isn't mineral or vegetable or dog or cat; nor is it part of mama, the way a leg or a tumor is part of mama.[15]

The heartbeat of the child in the womb is detectable as early as ten weeks after conception.[16] As Professor Ian Donald, an obstetrician of Glasgow University, said:

> This is not potential life, as some would have it—it is life indeed—human life at that. It is the same life, the same heart that might beat for another three score years and ten if you would but let it.[17]

The medical recognition that life begins at conception is not a novel theory or the private property of a few initiates in the higher reaches of the medical profession. Rather, it is such common knowledge that it has been stated simply as a matter of fact by responsible non-professional journals. On April 30, 1965, *Life* magazine published a startling photographic essay entitled, "Drama of Life Before Birth." The article featured actual photographs of the child in gestation, including one picture of a child, eighteen weeks after his conception, clearly sucking his thumb. Other pictures showed the child in various stages of development along the road to birth. The text of the article affirmed, as a simple fact, that "The birth of a human life really occurs at the moment the mother's egg cell is fertilized by one of the father's sperm cells." For the first eight weeks, until his permanent skeleton of bone begins to form, the child is commonly called an embryo, a Greek word meaning "to swell." Thereafter, he is usually called a fetus, a Latin word meaning "young one." At six and one half weeks, although the child weighs only one thirtieth of an ounce, he has all the internal organs he will ever have as an adult, including a little mouth with lips, a tongue, and buds for twenty milk teeth. At eight weeks his permanent skeleton has begun to form. By the time he is eighteen weeks old, the child even cries. He has a complete set of vocal cords, but since there is no air in the womb—he receives his oxygen from his mother's body—his crying makes no sound. At this time he can make a hard fist and inflicts scratches on himself with his fingernails.[18]

Newsweek magazine, in a detailed article on the "miracle" of birth, stated, "The perinatal period can be considered the first year of life—the period from conception through the nine months of pregnancy to the end of the first three months of infancy."[19] As one article recently said in advising expectant mothers, ". . . you not only provide half of your baby's heredity, you also furnish his total environment during the fast-growing, first nine months of his life."[20] The process of growth continues through the child's birth and beyond. Yet the abortion advocates would kill this child up to the twenty-fourth week of his life,[21] under the theory that he is not fully a human being but for the real reason that his life is inconvenient or disturbing to others or because those others deem him unfit to live. The result is to victimize this innocent child by the oldest technique known to the art of tyranny—arbitrarily defining a target class as outside the human race and therefore beyond the protection of the law.

The New York *Times Magazine* published an extensive study of the new medical specialty of fetology, by the noted medical writer James C. G. Conniff. The author described the moment of conception this way:

> At last, one—and only one—sperm penetrates the tough *zona pellucida*, the glass-clear membranous shell of the ovum, and joins its pronucleus with that of the egg. At that moment conception takes place and, scientists generally agree, a new life begins—silent, secret, unknown.[22]

New York City school officials announced in 1967 that they would begin the largest sex education program in the nation. The fifth-grade text unequivocally states, "Human life begins when the sperm cells of the father and the egg cells of the mother unite. This union is referred to as fertilization. For fertilization to take place and a baby to begin growing, the sperm cell must come in direct contact with the egg cell."[23] "Life begins when a sperm cell and an ovum (egg cell) unite," declares the text used in Evanston, Illinois, which has one of the most prominent sex education programs in the country.[24] "When an egg cell from the female and a sperm cell unite into a single cell," continues the Evanston text, "it is complete with 46 chromosomes and life begins." Even the Planned Parenthood Association, before it began its current campaign for abortion, admitted this scientific fact in a 1963 pamphlet:

> An abortion requires an operation. It kills the life of a baby after it has begun. It is dangerous to your life and health. It may make you sterile so that when you want a child you cannot have it. Birth control merely postpones the beginning of life.[25]

The highest court of New Jersey in 1960 summarized the state of scientific knowledge: "Medical authorities have long recognized that a child is in existence from the moment of conception."[26] These and other authorities bear witness to the scientific facts that the child in the womb is a human being from the moment of conception and that, in the words of the Planned Parenthood pamphlet, an abortion "kills the life of a baby after it has begun."

This finding of modern science, that life begins at conception, has been recognized in the development of the civil law of torts. As the New York Appellate Division said in 1953:

> We ought to be safe in this respect in saying that legal separability should begin where there is biological separability. We know something more of the actual process of conception and foetal development now than when some of the common-law cases were decided; and what we know makes it possible to demonstrate clearly that separability begins at conception. . . .

> If the child born after an injury sustained at any period of his prenatal life can prove the effect on him of the tort . . . we hold he makes out a right to recover.[27]

Other scientific authorities are analyzed in the District of Columbia case of Bonbrest v. Kotz, in which the federal court noted that, "From the viewpoint of the civil law and the law of property, a child en ventre sa mère is not only regarded as a human being, but as such from the moment of conception—which it is in fact."[28]

Dean William L. Prosser, in the basic textbook on the law of torts, discussed the unborn child's right to recover for an injury he sustained while in his mother's womb:

> So far as duty is concerned, if existence at the time is necessary, medical authority has recognized long since that the child is in existence from the moment of conception, and for many purposes its existence is recognized by the law. . . . So far as causation is concerned, there will certainly be cases in which there are difficulties of proof, but they are no more frequent, and the difficulties are no greater, than as to many other medical problems. All writers who have dicussed the problem have joined in condemning the old rule, in maintaining that the unborn child in the path of an automobile is as much a person in the street as the mother, and in urging that recovery should be allowed upon proper proof.[29]

Nor is the recognition in the law that life begins at conception limited to cases where the child is ultimately born alive. It is true that in most cases the law generally requires that an infant be born alive before he will have a remedy for tort or property rights that accrued to him during gestation. This negative reluctance to grant a remedy to the stillborn is founded upon the difficulty of computing damages and other administrative considerations. But this general tendency is by no means dispositive of the abortion issue. In fact, in recent years the courts have increasingly recognized the rights of the child in the womb whether ultimately born alive or not. Since 1949 the majority of states that have considered this question have ruled, for example, that a stillborn child may, through his representative, maintain a legal action for his wrongful death caused by injuries inflicted on him while he was in the womb.[30] A recent case in this direction was Raleigh Fitkin-Paul Morgan Memorial Hospital v. Anderson[31] in which the New Jersey court ruled that a child in the womb has the right to compel his mother to undergo a blood transfusion, to safeguard his life, even though the transfusion is contrary to the mother's religious principles. The New Jersey court in the Raleigh case affirmed "that the unborn child is entitled to the law's protection. . . ."[32] The Raleigh case incidentally raises another issue. In Raleigh the mother was required to undergo a transfusion for the benefit of the child in her womb. Some abortion advocates, as we shall see in the following discussion of Gleitman v. Cosgrove, contend that abortion of defectives actually confers a benefit on the defective child, who would be better off dead. If abortion is for the benefit of the child, could the mother be compelled to undergo an abortion just as the mother in Raleigh was compelled to submit to the transfusion? This result is entirely conceivable if we persist in our present disdain for the sanctity of life.

In 1967 the New Jersey court ruled directly on the rights of the unborn child in an abortion case. Jeffrey Gleitman was born in Jersey City on November 25, 1959, with substantial defects in sight, hearing, and speech. His mother had contracted German measles one month after she became pregnant with Jeffrey. When she was two months pregnant, she routinely consulted Drs. Cosgrove and Dolan, who practiced obstetrics and gynecology together in Jersey City. When she asked the doctors several times during the pregnancy about the effects of German measles, she "received a reassuring answer" each time. After the birth of Jeffrey, Mr. and Mrs. Gleitman sued the doctors to recover damages for the emotional effects and added financial burden caused to them by the doctors' failure to apprise them of the high risk of birth defects from German measles. The parents' theory was that, if the doctors had told them of the risks, they would have procured an abortion and thereby would have avoided their emotional and financial injury. There was no way that the birth defects could have been minimized during the pregnancy; the alternatives, therefore, were birth or abortion. More significantly, the parents sued on behalf of the infant Jeffrey. The court majority interpreted this claim as follows:

> The infant plaintiff is therefore required to say not that he should have been born without defects but that he should not have been born at all. . . . In other words, he claims that the conduct of defendants prevented his mother from obtaining an abortion which would have terminated his existence, and that his very life is "wrongful."[33]

The court rejected by a majority vote of 4–3 all the parents' claims, on their own behalf and on behalf of Jeffrey. The court majority went to the basic issue of the sanctity of life:

> It is basic to the human condition to seek life and hold on to it however heavily burdened. If Jeffrey could have been asked as to whether his life should be snuffed out before his full term of gestation could run its

course, our felt intuition of human nature tells us he would almost surely choose life with defects as against no life at all. "For the living there is hope, but for the dead there is none." Theocritus. . . .

The right to life is inalienable in our society. A court cannot say what defects should prevent an embryo from being allowed life such that denial of the opportunity to terminate the existence of a defective child in embryo can support a cause for action. Examples of famous persons who have had great achievements despite physical defects come readily to mind, and many of us can think of examples close to home. A child need not be perfect to have a worthwhile life.

We are not faced here with the necessity of balancing the mother's life against that of her child. The sanctity of the single human life is the decisive factor in this suit in tort. Eugenic considerations are not controlling. We are not talking here about the breeding of prize cattle. It may have been easier for the mother and less expensive for the father to have terminated the life of their child while he was an embryo, but these alleged detriments cannot stand against the preciousness of the single human life to support a remedy in tort. Cf. Jonathan Swift, "A Modest Proposal" in *Gulliver's Travels and Other Writings*, 488–496 (Modern Library ed., 1958).[34]

It was not without reason that the General Assembly of the United Nations voted that "the child by reason of his physical and mental immaturity, needs special safeguards and care, including appropriate legal protection, before as well as after birth."[35] To kill the child by abortion is a violation of his human right as well as of the basic tenets of the medical profession. As one doctor described his first sight, as a student, of an induced abortion, "To see what had been a live, pulsating and intriguing structure turned into an inert mass in the space of minutes, left one with an overwhelming sense of fear. . . . It convinced one that destruction of life could never be part of a doctor's role; it was against the very essence of what his mission is."[36]

Another interesting case was O'Beirne v. Kaiser Memorial Hospital. Presiding Judge George H. Barnett of the Superior Court of Santa Clara County, who rendered the initial decision in the matter, summarized the controversy in a letter as follows:

> Mr. O'Beirne brought an action for divorce against his wife on the grounds of mental cruelty. While the divorce was pending, they attempted a reconciliation during which time she became pregnant. Thereafter, they again separated. Without his knowledge, Mrs. O'Beirne applied for a therapeutic abortion under California's new Therapeutic Abortion Act. This law provides, insofar as this case is concerned, that Mrs. O'Beirne could apply for an abor-

tion to a duly approved hospital; the matter is reviewed by a panel of qualified physicians and a determination made to either grant or refuse the request. In this situation, the request was granted after Mrs. O'Beirne had been examined by the Chief of Psychiatry at Kaiser Hospital and also after an independent psychiatrist had recommended it as being necessary to preserve her mental health. Although the court was not concerned with the reasons for the medical determination, it appeared that the O'Beirnes had one child who was born with a club foot and they had experienced a miscarriage almost at full term in which the child was deformed with an enlarged abnormal head. It further appeared that Mrs. O'Beirne, because of this fact and her pending divorce, was possibly suicidal. . . .

Mr. O'Beirne, who is a Catholic, felt very strongly on both religious and moral grounds that the Therapeutic Abortion Act was unconstitutional as it deprived the unborn child of the right to be born and it also deprived the father of the right to have his child born without any due process by which was meant any proceeding to question the necessary determination.[37]

Mr. O'Beirne sued to prevent the abortion. Presiding Judge Barnett dismissed his complaint. The California State Supreme Court thereafter granted a peremptory hearing and denied Mr. O'Beirne's petition on a 5–2 decision with no opinion.

The O'Beirne case could have presented clearly the issue of the child's right not to be killed by abortion, since Mr. O'Beirne alleged that the abortion would deprive "the unborn child of the right to be born" as well as alleging his own rights as a father. However, Presiding Judge Barnett's decision plainly was based on his belief that the abortion was necessary to save the life of the mother. Although there was no reported opinion by Presiding Judge Barnett, he did state in his letter:

It was my decision that there were no constitutional rights as he claimed and even if there were, these were not absolute rights. Most constitutional rights are subject to various conditions and I felt that *whatever rights he might have had were inferior to the wife's right not to have her life jeopardized.* (Emphasis added.)

Clearly, Presiding Judge Barnett considered the case to involve an abortion required to save the life of the mother. He never squarely decided the issue of whether the abortion should be allowed if not necessary to save the life of the mother. Therefore, neither his decision nor the peremptory decision without opinion by the California State Supreme Court disturbs the proposition that the unborn child has a constitutional right to be born where an abortion is not required to save the life of his mother.

The most poignant argument for abortion can be made in cases where the pregnancy results from rape or incest. Opponents of abortion are often challenged by the claim that they would feel differently if a daughter of theirs had become pregnant as a result of a forcible rape. Dr. Morris S. Fond testified in favor of abortion before the New York legislative committee and he said:

> "I'll tell the members of this committee this: if my own daughter were raped by a mentally retarded maniac, I would see to it that either I or one of my colleagues would interrupt that pregnancy—abortion law or no. I probably would not be prosecuted or convicted, and I'm sure that each member of this committee would want similar treatment given to someone near or dear to him. To me this is the crux of the inequity in the present law."[38]

This argument is appealing until we realize that another human being—the innocent child in the womb—is involved. Joseph Fletcher, in his book, *Situation Ethics*, justifies abortion in the rape situation on the ground that, even if (as he does not concede) an abortion is a killing of a human being, it is not wrongful because the child and the rapist are both aggressors. Even if the rapist had been insane and therefore incapable of subjective intent, he contends, "self-defense legalism would have allowed the girl to kill her attacker." "The embryo," he says, "is no more innocent, no less an aggressor or unwelcome invader!"[39] Fletcher, however, is confused. While the rapist, if he were sane, was an aggressor, the child in gestation is clearly not. According to Webster's Collegiate Dictionary, "Aggressive implies the disposition to dominate, sometimes by indifference to others' rights, but now, more often, by determined, forceful prosecution of one's ends." Whatever the right of the girl to kill an aggressor attempting to rape her, it cannot be said that the child conceived by the rape is also an aggressor. For he obviously cannot entertain the subjective intent requisite to aggression.

But the critical issue here is not whether the child in the womb is an "aggressor." The right of self-defense does not depend upon the existence of subjective malevolence in the attacker. The attacker need not be an aggressor in that sense. Otherwise, the girl would have no right to kill an insane man attempting to rape her by force. She does, however, have that right as a matter of self-defense. The right of an innocent person to defend himself against deadly personal attack or against the commission of a felony upon his person is so highly valued that the perpetrator of the attack forfeits his own immunity to personal injury and death even where the perpetrator is insane and therefore lacking in malevolence. For the goal is not punishment of a personally culpable attacker but reasonable self-defense by an innocent victim. However, this extraordinary right to inflict death in defending oneself against attack can be justified only where an active menace is presented to the victim by the action of the attacker. The rule of self-defense is for "the protection of one's self, of others and of property against *unlawful conduct*." It "governs the use of defensive force against *felonious attack*," as it was described in the American Law Institute's comments on the Model Penal Code.[40] It is wholly inappropriate as a justification for killing the innocent, passive, wholly defenseless child in the womb.

If it be argued that the rapist's child in his victim's womb presents an excruciating menace to the mental and physical health, as well as the social standing, of the unwilling mother, two things should be said in reply. For one thing, the child in the womb is wholly passive. He is not an attacker. If violence is to be done, it must proceed entirely from his mother. Secondly, he does not pose a threat to the mother's life. If the mother is to be allowed to kill this passive child because his mere existence is a less than mortal menace to her physical, mental, or social health, then we will have verged into killing for convenience. If we are to have it, let us call it that and argue it on its proper foundation. It wholly distorts the meaning of language to say that the proven concepts of self-defense support the killing of a passive infant for the less than mortal welfare—i.e., the convenience—of the mother.

To legalize abortion in pregnancies caused by rape would affect only an infinitesimal number of cases. This is particularly so, since even Catholic teaching permits measures to be taken within a reasonable time following a rape, which have the effect of preventing conception.[41] In any event, the rape issue is an emotional lure used by those who seek a general relaxation of the abortion laws. It would be far better and far more humane in rape and incest cases if we directed our energies and the full resources of society toward helping both the mother and the child rather than revert to the primitive cruelty of killing an innocent human being.

The case for abortion where the pregnancy resulted from incest is even weaker than in the rape situation. In incest, the impregnating intercourse presumably was not accomplished by physical force against an unwilling victim. If it were, or if the victim were under the age of consent, we would have the rape problem. If the girl consented to the intercourse, the abortion amounts to nothing more than giving her a chance to repent her folly. Repentance is a good thing, but not so good as to justify the taking of an innocent life.

It is frequently urged, on behalf of abortion, that legalization will enable mothers to have their abortions under safe hospital conditions rather than at the hands of quack abortionists in dangerous surroundings.

On the contrary, liberalization of abortion laws increases rather than decreases the number of illegal abortions. The experience of Japan and Sweden, where illegal as well as legal abortions have increased since the liberalization of the abortion laws, argues convincingly to this point. Professor Robert M. Byrn observes that "liberalization of the law makes abortion more culturally acceptable. Women who might never have thought of an abortion now believe that they have a right to one—even though their reasons for seeking it may be legally insufficient. The result is an entirely new (and perhaps larger) clientele for the criminal abortionist."[42] Legalization of abortion also tends to diminish the use of contraceptives. Increasingly, women regard abortion as a "fail safe" birth control technique, enabling them to avoid the inconvenience of contraceptives. In Japan, women who are active sexually and don't want babies find it simpler to have abortions approximately every eight months until sterility sets in.[43] When abortions are legalized, the pregnancies tend to increase and therefore so do abortions. On the contrary, the way to reduce illegal abortions is to enforce the law to the utmost. Between 1946 and 1953 an intensified campaign of prosecutions resulted in a substantial reduction in the number of criminal abortions in New York City.[44] Illegal abortion should be viewed mainly as a crime problem. When we are faced with an increase of crime, we ought not to legalize the crime, at least not where human lives are involved. Abortion laws can be enforced and they should be. Moreover, they should be enforced as well against those who, acting out of a misguided humanitarianism, refer pregnant women to cooperating doctors for illegal abortions.[45]

Abortion, too, involves a substantial physical risk to the mother wherever it is performed. In addition to the 100% mortality for the unborn child, estimates of maternal mortality in therapeutic abortion run as high as 5%. The Council of England's Royal College of Obstetricians and Gynecologists reported in the *British Medical Journal:*

> Those without specialist knowledge, and these include members of the medical profession, are influenced in adopting what they regard as a humanitarian attitude to the induction of abortion by a failure to appreciate what is involved. They tend to regard induction of abortion as a trivial operation free from risk. In fact, even to the expert working in the best conditions, the removal of an early pregnancy after dilating the cervix can be difficult, and is not infrequently accompanied by serious complications. This is particularly true in the case of the woman pregnant for the first time. For women who have a serious medical indication for termination of pregnancy, induction of abortion is extremely hazardous and its risks need to be weighed carefully against those involved in leaving the pregnancy undisturbed. Even for the relatively healthy woman, however, the dangers are considerable.[46]

The current proposals would legalize abortion where continuance of the pregnancy would endanger the physical or mental health of the mother. The proponents tell us that the revised laws would legalize at most only 20% of the illegal abortions now performed. But they underestimate the potential of their proposals. One New York doctor boasts of having committed more than 30,000 illegal abortions.[47] Imagine what the new law would do for his practice. It would open the door to abortion on demand, or for mere convenience, through elastic interpretations of "mental health." Indeed, there is reason to believe that abortion on demand is the goal of at least some of the proponents of liberalized abortion. One feminist group, the National Organization for Women, wants to repeal the abortion laws as a simple matter of freedom for women to decide whether to bear children.[48] The president of the New York chapter of NOW advocates abortion as part of an over-all program of female emancipation that includes the abolition of the family unit and the raising of children in communes. The American Civil Liberties Union claims that "every woman, as a matter of her right to the enjoyment of life, liberty and privacy," should be free to have an abortion at the hands of a licensed physician until the child is viable (usually twenty weeks) and that all laws imposing criminal penalties for abortion should be repealed.[49]

Abortion really tends to injure the health of the mother rather than promote it. There is no causal relation established between pregnancy and mental illness and, even if there were, there is no proof that termination of the pregnancy solves any existing problem. Incidentally, in one survey, 92% of the women surveyed who had an abortion under the liberal Japanese laws stated that they felt guilty about it.[50] Another survey showed extensive guilt feelings in women after they had abortions. Many were troubled by the sight of small children, experienced a feeling of emptiness, and longed for the child whose death they had obtained.[51] It is possible, too, to quote authorities such as Dr. J. Grant Harrison of New York, who concluded "that the more severe the patient's psychiatric illness, the more she would react to abortion, or, the greater risk of psychic sequelae after abortion. . . . It is interesting to note," he said, "that the two highest suicide rates for women are found in Japan (14%) and Hungary (17%), two countries where abortion rates legalized and illegal are highest."[52] But surveys and statistics can be deceptive. Instead, common sense and experience are reliable guides in judging a matter so basic. It is folly to suppose that a mother can deliberately destroy her young and go blithely on with no untoward consequence of mind or conscience. Dr. Mary Calderone declared her opposition to indiscriminate abortion and said that "aside from the fact that abortion is the taking of a life, I am mindful of what was brought out by our psychiatrists, that in almost every case abortion, whether legal or illegal, is a traumatic experience that may have severe kickbacks later on."[53]

Abortion is worse than a neglect, or even a callous indifference, to the rights of others. It involves the calculated destruction of a helpless one committed by the strongest bonds of nature to the love and protection of the mother who wilfully kills him. Perhaps the Roman poet Ovid best revealed the reason for the "kickbacks" when he described abortion as a depraved act unworthy even of a savage beast:

> Women, why will you thrust and pierce with an instrument and kill your children yet unborn? That neither the tigress has done in the jungles of

Armenia, nor did the lioness ever have it in her heart to destroy her unborn young.[54]

The impeccable and very clinical advocates of abortion "reform" present their case as if an abortion were a bloodless and pleasant exercise. One would almost think that the abortionist simply waves his magic wand and the child in the womb obligingly disappears. In fact, however, a routine abortion is a bloody mess, literally a blood bath. Professor Ian Donald, as obstetrician of Glasgow University, had this to say about it:

> I must resist the temptation to tell you the nasty details of the operation employed to terminate [pregnancies]. In a few minutes, I would have you vomiting in the aisles. Professor Norman Norris described it as a hemorrhagic exercise in destruction—a masterly understatement. Can you wonder then at the built-in resistance of most gynaecologists to performing it. . . .
>
> Make no mistake about it. An unborn baby, even a very small one, can put up a determined fight for life. An abortion can be born alive and can kick and go on kicking for quite a long time. It is not difficult to see this as a sort of slow murder. On the other hand, the baby can be killed while still inside. Is there so much difference? The intention is the same.[55]

When a woman desires to be sterilized at the same time that she has her abortion, the abortion is usually performed by hysterotomy, by cutting the abdomen and lifting the baby out as in the classic Caesarean section technique of childbirth. At the stage at which this type of abortion is carried out, the child is well formed, with its limbs and organs quite recognizable. Frequently the child cries and must be either laid aside to cry himself to death or destroyed by the doctor and his assistants. Mrs. Jill Knight, a Member of the British Parliament, observed:

> In Sweden, if the child has not been killed by the operation, they drown it in a bucket like a kitten. The child will kick miserably until it dies.
>
> They also do experiments on aborted babies. Put them in simulated wombs and feed them through the cord, poking them now and again to see if they are still alive.
>
> Why not, I was told—no one wants these babies.[56]

Another method of abortion is dilation of the cervix and curettage of the uterus, wherein the womb is "evacuated" by cutting and scraping away the child, the placenta, and the sac. Listen to Dr. Alan Guttmacher, a leading proponent of abortion, describe the technique:

A sharp curette is then inserted to the top of the fundus with very little force, for it is during this phase that the uterus is most likely to be perforated. Moderate force can be safely exerted on the down stroke. The whole uterine cavity is curetted with short strokes, by visualizing a clock and making a stroke at each hour. The curette is then withdrawn several times bringing out pieces of placenta and sac. A small ovum forceps is then inserted and the cavity tonged for tissue, much like an oysterman tonging for oysters. . . . In pregnancies beyond the seventh week, *fetal parts are recognizable as they are removed piecemeal.*[57]

When Dr. Guttmacher refers clinically to "fetal parts," he means arms, legs, a head, and the various other "parts" that, moments before, comprised a living human body. Incidentally, some doctors, including Dr. A. W. Liley of New Zealand and Professor James Scott of Leeds, both leading experts on intra-uterine transfusion, are convinced from their experiments that the child at the stage when abortions are usually performed can feel pain.[58]

Permissive abortion inevitably engenders a callous disregard for life. Life is cheap when abortion is free, as seen from the case in Japan where a young mother was anticipating her first child. She visited a local private clinic for a prenatal examination. After speaking with a doctor, she was shown into a treatment room and placed under anesthesia. When she regained her senses, she discovered to her horror that an abortion had been routinely performed.[59]

The day is coming, however, when abortions will not be messy. Soviet scientists claim to have developed an "easy and harmless method of abortion by suction."[60] Scientists in Sweden and elsewhere are nearing perfection of abortion pills. There is a pill in prospect that the woman would have to take only once a month, toward the end of her menstrual cycle. It would induce menstruation before the woman even knew whether she was pregnant. If she were pregnant, the child would be aborted, but the woman could more easily rationalize away any feelings of guilt since she would not know whether she had been pregnant.[61]

In a way, it is a good thing that abortion pills are being developed. They will present the moral issue of the right to life starkly and inescapably. As the new science of fetology reveals more and more about the unborn child, it will become clear to all, beyond the shadow of a doubt, that an abortion at any time after the instant of conception is the killing of a human being. Today the morality of contraception, whether mechanically or by contraceptive pills, is clouded in ambiguity for some people. But when the woman holds in her hand an abortion pill, designed specifically to terminate an existing even if unknown pregnancy, the moment of truth will be at hand. If she takes it, she will be, in her own conscience, a murderess, whether in fact she was pregnant or not. Unless the present trend is reversed, abortion is destined to replace contraception as the primary means of birth control. If we as a people adopt the abortion pill as a way of life, as we seem to have adopted the contraceptive pill, we shall be on the road to extinction and perdition. These clear-cut choices are coming. They lend a special urgency to our efforts to rouse people to their clear responsibilities and to an appreciation of the sanctity of every human life.

The abortion advocates would further ordain that a child can be legally killed when there is a "substantial risk" that he will be born with "physical or mental abnormalities." How, we are entitled to ask, would such eugenic engineering differ from the indefensible ideas and techniques that prevailed in Nazi Germany a generation ago? The answer, in principle, is that they would differ not at all. And the logically inescapable step beyond abortion to kill the defective unborn child is infanticide to kill the defective infant after he is born. Indeed, such abortion is even more intolerable than infanticide, which is so obviously a regression to primitive and inhuman ways. Infanticide does not imperil the mother's life and it has an element of certainty about it—you need kill only those children whom you know, after birth, to be defective. But when we kill, by abortion, an unborn child because he may turn out to be defective when born, we risk killing an unborn child who would not be defective. There are indications that science will soon be able to detect birth defects with accuracy while the child is still in the womb. At that point, we shall face the moral issue here unequivocally. We can blunt the abortionist's argument today by pointing out that, when he advocates abortion if the mother contracted German measles at an early stage of the pregnancy, he willingly kills four healthy children for the sake of destroying the 20% who are affected by the disease. But we cannot rest on this argument, as we cannot concede a right to kill even an admittedly defective child. Rabbi Immanuel Jakobovits, Chief Rabbi of England, put the issue in perspective when he said, "Human life being infinite in value, its sanctity is bound to be entirely unaffected by the absence of any or all mental faculties or by any bodily defects: any fraction of infinity still remains infinite."[62] Society has made significant progress in the treatment of retarded, deformed and defective persons. Would it not be better to devote our energies and resources to improving the chances of these people to lead productive and useful lives, instead of sentencing them to death for specious reasons that really mask a selfish refusal to bother with them? As Mrs. Jill Knight, M.P. put it:

> Can anyone who has seen and talked to blind people or spastic paraplegics or even mentally handicapped people put his hand on his heart and say: "These people have no right to live"?
> I firmly believe they have such a right and that they find their own ways to enjoy life's blessings.
> Nazi Germany, of course, thought the way this Bill thinks. Only physically perfect specimens were the Reich's anointed.
> *Any country which adopts this creed is not a Christian country.*[63]

The simple fact is that abortion of defective children is a form of involuntary euthanasia. The principle is the same in either case. Once we have defined a human being outside of the human race because he is too young—that is, he has not yet lived nine months since his conception—there is no obstacle in principle to defining him out because he is too old. And if the child in the womb can be made an outlaw because he may be defective, and therefore a useless burden on society, so too can the senile, the paralytics, and the "useless eaters." Dr. Frederick Wentz, president of a Lutheran seminary in Ohio, has voiced a rationale under which defectives of any age could be regarded as not human and therefore liable to be destroyed. After noting that "there is no way of telling when" human life begins in the womb, he continued:

> Actually there does not seem to be any clear way of telling *if* that event has taken place until the child itself makes observable human responses (perhaps in the act of calling other people by name). Some children, who were seemingly normally brought to birth, never achieve distinctly human responses. In such cases we remain in entire mystery as to whether God willed a human life into being or did not.[64]

This so-called eugenic abortion to eliminate defective children would have deprived the world of a Charles Steinmetz and other people of great stature. As one observer said, "On a similar supposition there would have been no Abraham Lincoln, as his mother, Nancy Hanks, was the result of an affair between a poor, shiftless girl without education or means or morals, and a stranger from thither side of the mountain."[65] And there is the familiar story of one doctor asking another: "About the terminating of a pregnancy, I want your opinion. The father was syphilitic. The mother tuberculous. Of the four children born, the first was blind, the second died, the third was deaf and dumb, the fourth also tuberculous. What would you have done?" "I would have ended the pregnancy." "Then you would have murdered Beethoven."[66]

More ominously, eugenic abortion would open the way to the systematic elimination of defective or "inferior" people as a matter of government policy. If we say that a child in the womb is inferior because he may be defective, then the defective person who has already been born must also be inferior and therefore subject to destruction as a burden on others and the state. And if we abide a decision that a blind or retarded child is inferior, and therefore liable to death, what principled defense can we raise to an official judgment that a child is inferior because he or his parents are Jewish or Negro or Catholic? On what logical ground could we resist the "mercy killing," Nazi style, of adult incurables, defectives, "useless eaters," and political undesirables? Once we begin to define human beings out of the human race and cast them beyond the protection of the law, there is no durable safeguard short of an ultimate tyranny. We shall examine these implications in detail in the next chapter.

The drive to liberalize abortion laws cannot be viewed in an academic vacuum. Many abortion advocates conceive it primarily as a measure for population control. Dr. Robert Hall of Columbia University, president of the impossibly named Association for Humane Abortion—how can an abortion be humane to the child?— acknowledged that "birth control in its broadest sense includes contraception, sterilization, and abortion, no one of which will suffice alone."[67] When Governor Rockefeller of New York first proposed a relaxation of the abortion laws in 1966, he included the abortion proposal in the family planning section of his State of the

State message to the legislature. Abortion is the single most effective method of birth limitation. It was abortion that succeeded in reducing the birth rate in Japan to a point where the Japanese people are not even replacing themselves. In Hungary there are 1400 legal abortions for every 1000 live births.[68] Dr. Nicholas Naradi, a former Hungarian Finance Minister, recently predicted that his people would cease to exist within a hundred and fifty years.[69] Communist Rumania, in 1966, abandoned the liberal abortion policy it had pursued for more than two decades. Abortions were easily obtainable and the result was a serious drop in the birth rate. To arrest the population decline, the Communist authorities made it a criminal offense to perform an abortion or for women to undergo one, with few limited exceptions.[70]

Certain Negro leaders have complained that some federal programs to curtail births are really genocidal in their operation against the Negro people. In some instances, at least, there has been indirect coercion of welfare recipients to practice contraception. If abortion laws are generally relaxed, we may fairly expect that case workers will be authorized to inform welfare clients of their rights in the area. Further, it is easy to foresee the practice degenerating into implicit coercion of welfare recipients to procure abortions. Such a technique would be fully in accord with a materialistic view of life. And the only way to prevent it is to foster an uncompromising reverence for life that will brook no subordination of innocent life to any considerations of policy or convenience.

The current laws generally permit abortion where it is necessary to preserve the life of the mother. In fact the medical indications for abortion to save the life of the mother have practically ceased to exist. As Dr. André E. Hellegers of Johns Hopkins University concluded, "Medicine has come to a point where it is almost a truism to say that no mother requires an abortion for the *instant* saving of her life."[71] This view was seconded by Dr. R. J. Heffernan of Tufts University, who said, "Anyone who performs a therapeutic abortion is either ignorant of modern medical methods of treating the complications of pregnancy or is unwilling to take time to use them."[72] Yet under these restrictive laws, some 10,000 "legal" abortions are performed in the United States every year. Obviously there ought to be a stricter application of the laws that allow abortion only to save the life of the mother. Too frequently doctors evade these laws by falsely certifying that the abortion is necessary to prevent the suicide of the mother. In a typical year about 80% of the 800 or so legal abortions performed in New York City are performed to avert suicide. "Yet," said Dr. Robert Hall, an abortion advocate, "we know that all these women are not suicidal. The abortions are done to preserve maternal health, not life."[73] Too often a dominant factor in the doctor's decision is money. When an abortion is considered, the life of the child is placed in the hands of a doctor who, because of his interest in earning a fee for the abortion, is hardly a disinterested judge. Money talks. And when the mother has it, the money can too easily say that an innocent child must die. Even Dr. Alan Guttmacher of Planned Parenthood acknowledged this unpleasant reality:

> In borderline cases and all too frequently in cases which are not borderline, the patient's prestige and money are very vocal in getting an undesired pregnancy terminated. I am loath to admit it, but far too often a minor difficulty is stretched into a major abnormality for the right person.[74]

When the law authorizes an abortion that is really necessary to save the life of the mother, there is a parity of values that admits of debate. It is one life for another life and it is possible to argue that the common-law principles of necessity authorize the taking of the life of the innocent child in the womb when it is directly and inescapably necessary to the preservation of the very life of another. On the other hand, even in that case it is sounder to conclude that the common-law principles ought not to be stretched so far as to sanction the killing of such an entirely passive, helpless, and innocent victim. As one commentary states:

> It is generally held that the law in no event recognizes the right of one person, however dire the situation, to kill an innocent person so that he himself may survive, and such killing is held felonious; this is the situation which might arise in a shipwreck or in similar circumstances, where there is insufficient food or means of transport. There was a dictum in United States v. Holmes, 1 Wall. Jr. 1, Fed. Cas. No. 15,383, that such homicide is not felonious if lots are drawn to determine who shall die; this doctrine, however, was specifically discredited in Regina v. Dudley, (Eng.) L.R.Q.B.Div. 273, 15 Cox Cr.624, and the doctrine of homicide by necessity has been generally repudiated by English and American courts.[75]

It can be argued, therefore, that abortion ought not to be permitted even where it is necessary to save the life of the mother. The existing laws that permit such abortions, then, should be repealed. And this position is sound, although the issue is fairly debatable because there is a parity there of one life for another. However, even under the assumption that the existing laws ought to be repealed, there is no need to do so. For in fact it is no longer medically necessary to perform an abortion to save the very life of the mother. The immediate remedy is to enforce the existing law to stop the performance of abortions under the fraudulent pretense that they are necessary to save the life of the mother.

But whatever arguments can be made for abortion when there is a parity of one life for another, no such arguments can be made for abortion when an innocent life is to be sacrificed for the convenience of others or because those others consider that life inferior. If we are to affirm the sanctity of innocent life, as we ought, we at least should protect that life against forfeiture for any reason less than the direct preservation of the life of another innocent person. If this interpretation has the effect of reducing "legal" abortions to the vanishing point, so much the better.

So-called therapeutic abortion cannot be justified by analogy to capital punishment or conscription. In capital punishment, the life of the criminal is taken for the good of the state and to save the lives of others. But the criminal has forfeited his right to life by his own guilty aggression. The child whose life is ended by an abortion, however, is wholly innocent. Similarly, we justify conscription by positing a civic duty to offer one's life as a sacrifice in defense of his fellow citizens and the state. The end, the very survival of the state and perhaps civilization, justifies the imposition of such a duty on an innocent civilian. But the abortionist would "conscript" the child in the womb for a lesser good, i.e., the mere convenience of others, eugenics, or population limitation, which cannot justify the drafting of the innocent child in the womb to certain death. In the opinion of Dr. John Rock, a leading Catholic proponent of the contraceptive pill, ". . . the dignity of being human can demand of the embryos the same responsibility to the preservation of the human race—and hence a willingness to die—that we now demand of soldiers. They go out equally unquestioning, to die on the battlefields for the same purpose."[76] Dr. Rock's willingness to draft the child in the womb leaves no room for the child to raise a conscientious objection to his own destruction.

Our task is to promote responsibility by affirming the sanctity of life. Implicit in that affirmation is the certainty that the life of the lowliest, or the smallest, or the youngest, is worth as much as the life of the greatest. When the issue is drawn on the line of abortion, we must defend a person we cannot see. But he is there and his innocent life must be protected as fully as our own. For the issue is life itself and if we fail the child in the womb, we can hardly be assured that we shall succeed in our defense of the defective child in an institution, of the insane in an asylum, of the senile in a hospital, or of the politically undesirable in a concentration camp. Dr. Joseph De Lee of the University of Chicago emphasized in 1940 the importance of that one life in the womb:

> All doctors (except abortionists) feel that the principles of the sanctity of human life, held since the time of the ancient Jews and Hippocrates and stubbornly defended by the Catholic Church, are correct. And we are pained when placed before the necessity of sacrificing it. At the present time, when rivers of blood and tears of innocent men, women and children are flowing in most parts of the world, it seems silly to be contending over the right to live of an unknowable atom of human flesh in the uterus of a woman. No, it is not silly. On the contrary, it is of transcendent importance that there be in this chaotic world one high spot, however small, which is against the deluge of immorality that is sweeping over us. That we the medical profession hold to the principle of the sacredness of human life and of the right of the individual even though unborn is proof that humanity is not yet lost and that we may ultimately obtain salvation.[77]

4

EUTHANASIA

"She's out of her misery now. I shot her. She was in great pain. She begged me to do it." With these words, Robert Waskin, a twenty-two-year-old college senior, walked out of his mother's hospital room in Chicago on August 8, 1967.

The mother, fifty-two years old, was suffering from incurable leukemia. At the time of her death she was in the hospital on account of an overdose of sleeping pills given to her by Robert. But her leukemia had caused her to be hospitalized five times in the last two months of her life. She "always was in great pain," said Daniel Waskin, her widower and father of the slayer. The elder Waskin confirmed that his wife had pleaded with him and Robert "many times" to put her out of her misery. As Robert was charged with murder, the father refused to condemn him and maintained that his wife had died of leukemia. "That's what she was dying from and that's what she died of as far as I'm concerned," he said. "I don't think he murdered her. The boy loved his mother very much. I know he meant to do right." As Robert was led away in handcuffs, his mother's sister forgivingly cradled his face in her hands, kissed him, and said, "I love you." Robert was indicted for murder by the grand jury. Robert's trial is pending at this writing, in October 1968.

This was no ordinary murder. It was an act of euthanasia, a mercy killing. The term "euthanasia" derives from the Greek words meaning "easy or painless death." It can be voluntary or involuntary. Voluntary euthanasia consists of administering death to one who asks for it. It is really assisted suicide, but it differs from the usual meaning of suicide, in that the euthanasia victim (or beneficiary, depending on your point of view) is already incurably ill and desires to die. To the extent that his mother pleaded with him to end her life, Robert Waskin committed voluntary euthanasia.

Involuntary euthanasia, on the other hand, does not depend on the consent or request of the person to be killed. Rather, it consists of dispatching persons who are in such condition that they would welcome death but are physically or mentally incapable of asking for it. Or it involves the elimination of defective or hopelessly ill persons who, whether they desire to die or not, are judged by the killer, or by those entrusted with the power of decision, to be better off dead.

In English-speaking countries euthanasia is murder or manslaughter in the eyes of the law and no mitigation is allowed on account of consent of the victim or the compassionate motives of the killer. In some countries, e.g., Germany, Switzerland, Norway, these factors are allowed to mitigate the penalty. Even in Anglo-Saxon countries, however, sympathetic juries routinely soften the penalties imposed on mercy killers, often by verdicts inconsistent with the law. When Louis Repouille chloroformed his "incurably imbecile," blind, and bedridden thirteen-year-old son to death in 1939, he was convicted of second-degree manslaughter and given a suspended sentence. Later a United States federal court denied Repouille's petition for naturalization on the ground that the mercy killing showed he was not of "good moral character." Judge Learned Hand, in upholding the denial of naturalization, described the inconsistency of the lenient verdict in Repouille's mercy-killing trial:

> There being no lawful means of accomplishing an end, which they believe to be righteous in itself, there have always been conscientious persons who feel no scruple in acting in defiance of a law which is repugnant to their personal convictions, and who even regard as martyrs those who suffer by doing so. In our own history it is only necessary to recall the Abolitionists. It is reasonably clear that the jury which tried Repouille did not feel any moral repulsion at his crime. Although it was inescapably murder in the first degree, not only did they bring in a verdict that was flatly in the face of the facts and utterly absurd—for manslaughter in the second degree presupposes that the killing has not been deliberate—but they coupled even that with a recommendation which showed that in substance they wished to exculpate the offender. Moreover, it is also plain, from the sentence which he imposed, that the judge could not have seriously disagreed with their recommendation.[1]

The contemporary movement to legalize euthanasia was organized in England in 1936 with the formation of the Voluntary Euthanasia Legalisation Society. In 1938 the Euthanasia Society of America was founded. Similar groups exist on state and local levels. These organizations have restricted themselves formally to the advocacy of voluntary euthanasia. So far they have not succeeded in securing enactment of their proposals.

Generally, three different techniques have been suggested to legalize voluntary euthanasia. One was originally introduced in the House of Lords in 1936. This bill, an outgrowth of the campaign of the Voluntary Euthanasia Legalisation Society, required that the patient, who must be twenty-one years old, sane, and suffering from an incurable and painful terminal illness, execute a formal euthanasia application with two witnesses. The application would go to an official "euthanasia referee," with medical certificates from the attending physician and another specially qualified physician. The referee would be required to interview the patient. If the referee was satisfied that the requirements for euthanasia had been met, the killing would be performed by a licensed euthanasor in the presence of an official witness, who must be a justice of the peace, lawyer, doctor, nurse, or minister of religion. The Euthanasia Society of America has advanced a similar proposal that requires the approval of the courts before euthanasia can be administered.

Apart from the defects they have in common with all voluntary euthanasia proposals, these elaborate procedures, with their macabre attention to formalities, have a weakness all their own. For by institutionalizing a civic ritual of death, they would make it no longer an intensely private affair between man and his Maker, but rather an impersonal episode in the functioning of a novel but ultimately ordinary bureaucracy. Perhaps their major vice is that they would tend to make euthanasia routine and even a bore. More importantly, there is no necessary relation between intricacy of procedure and justice. Even if we assumed that a patient had a right to be euthanatized, we would not assuredly improve the credibility of his decision by filtering it through layers of progressively more impersonal functionaries.

A second line of relaxation has been suggested by Glanville Williams, a leading advocate of voluntary euthanasia. He would avoid the cumbersome machinery of euthanasia referees or committees, and would instead relieve the physician of responsibility if he acted in good faith. The Williams proposal "would provide that no medical practitioner should be guilty of an offense in respect of an act done intentionally to accelerate the death of a patient who is seriously ill, unless it is proved that the act was not done in good faith and with the consent of the patient for the purpose of saving him from severe pain in an illness believed to be of an incurable and fatal character."[2]

Williams' proposal is not limited to cases in which death is imminent but would sanction euthanasia in the early stages of an illness "believed" to be incurable and fatal. He does not specify whose belief it must be, the doctor's or the patient's, nor does he require even that the belief be reasonable. Williams is clearly writing a blank check for administered suicide.

The basic functional weakness of Williams' idea is the enormous power it gives to doctors. Some doctors are highly skilled, some are incompetent, and most are in between. In terms of their integrity, a similar variance obtains. Nor can we say that all doctors are gifted with the delicacy of understanding and the compassion that a euthanasor, in Williams' conception, would have to bring to his task.

The Williams suggestion, incidentally, is not limited to adults. Rather, "The use that may be made of my proposed measure in respect of patients who are minors is best left to the good sense of the doctor, taking into account, as he always does, the wishes of the parents as well as those of the child."[3] In this respect, the plan verges into involuntary euthanasia, to the extent that the desires of the parents and the doctor are implemented without the express consent of the child. And where the child is below the age at which he can make a reasonable judgment, the euthanasia is clearly involuntary.

A third method of liberalization[4] would retain the legal prohibitions against euthanasia. But it would ameliorate them by having the legislature create different classes of homicide with mercy killings on a lower level of severity, or provide that the punishment would be lessened by proof of a benevolent motive. The objective of this idea has already been attained by juries who render compassionate verdicts in poignant mercy-killing cases and by judges who moderate their sentences. This informal extension of mercy operates in a fairly predictable and consistent manner. However, it would be unwise to confirm it formally in the statutory law. If the law were to affirm that consent of the victim or subjective benevolence of the killer can mitigate the crime of murder, it would formally encourage even involuntary euthanasia and would promote the deceptive assertion of benevolent motives in cases of outright selfish murder. Such a weakening of the strictures against homicide would further diminish the reverence for innocent life which it is the duty of the law to uphold.

The three techniques for legalizing voluntary euthanasia—petition to the euthanasia referee, exculpation of the doctor acting in good faith, and formal reduction of the legal sanction—have their own special weaknesses. But there are grave objections to the very idea of voluntary euthanasia itself. Those objections can be raised on a utilitarian level as well as on a plane of essential principle.

All voluntary euthanasia schemes have a number of practical deficiencies in common.[5] These deficiencies increase the chance of mistake or misinterpretation of a patient's intent, to a point where the risk ought to be unacceptable even to those who favor mercy killing in principle.

For one thing, what about the reality of the consent? Voluntary euthanasia depends for its justification on an urgent and considered request for it by the patient. Yet in a terminal illness it is difficult to gauge the validity of such a request. It would be highly unusual for any person, even racked by painful illness, to entertain a fixed and resolute purpose to die. The moods and physical condition of a patient can vary from day to day and even from hour to hour. Obviously one ought not to support euthanasia based upon a request uttered only once by a patient. "I wish I were dead," has become almost an American idiom, suitable for use in accident wards or aspirin commercials. How many times, then, would the request have to be repeated and for how long should the patient be required to persevere in his fixed determination to die? In order to evaluate the request, would it not be necessary to canvass statements made by the patient prior to his illness? We are dealing with a decision as irrevocable as any can be. Ought we, then, to credit a patient's request for euthanasia when he had never uttered such a desire before his illness? Or when he had spoken against suicide

—voluntary euthanasia is assisted suicide—or belonged to a religious body opposed to suicide?

If we suppose a patient who had, while in good health, repeatedly said that he would rather die by euthanasia than endure a painful terminal illness, we would have a seemingly strong verification of his deathbed request for euthanasia. But it is one thing to voice the casual desire for euthanasia when death seems far away and the whole matter academic. It is quite another thing to request your own death when the time for cocktail-party conjecture is past and that request will literally cause your life to end. Surely no earlier, vagrant expressions in favor of euthanasia can suffice to replace a hard-core, verified desire to die when the illness actually strikes. At most, those earlier expressions can only corroborate the deathbed request. But if that deathbed request is itself inherently unreliable, no amount of corroboration should operate to give it the legal effect of a death warrant.

The fact is, however, that deathbed requests for euthanasia are indeed inherently unreliable. Presumably, the patient would be a candidate for voluntary euthanasia because his illness is terminal and unbearably painful. We can hardly expect a person in agonizing pain to make a detached and deliberate judgment that he ought to die then and there. Generally, however, the patient would be heavily dosed with narcotics or other analgesics. Surely we cannot credit a death request made while under the influence of drugs. If the drugs are withdrawn, the patient generally experiences an intensification of the pain that presumably had been growing unbearable even with the administration of the drugs. Surely we ought not to credit a death request made during such a temporary withdrawal of pain-killing drugs. In either case, whether drugged or racked with pain beyond the point of endurance, the patient ought not to be entrusted with the responsibility of buying a new car, let alone signing himself into eternity.

Incidentally, in a number of cases courts have denied probate to wills when the testator, at the time of execution, was so heavily under the influence of pain-killing drugs that he no longer had the capacity to make a will.[6] Whether or not a testator has the requisite capacity depends upon the facts of the particular case as meticulously proven to the satisfaction of the court. But the caution of the law in this area ought to be warning enough against a simplistic reliance upon a patient's expressed desire to die.

If the illness is terminal but not unbearably painful and does not require stupefying drugs, the patient may still ask to die "because my family would be better off without me to burden them." His request, it is true, would be more credible than if he were drugged or suffering extremely. But, as the product of despondence and even despair, it is not worthy of fatal reliance. The incurably ill person who asks to die may not be so deranged as to be legally insane. But the fact that the law would hold him responsible for any crimes he might commit does not mean that the law should formally ratify his request to die. His expressed desire is so contrary to the instinct of nature that it would be imprudent and perilous for the law to give it operative effect.

Apart from the inherent unreliability of a patient's request to die, other factors increase the chance of error to the point where voluntary euthanasia becomes pragmatically untenable. Doctors are not infallible in their diagnoses. Clearly, voluntary euthanasia should be limited to incurable cases. But if we premise it on a diagnosis of incurability, we impose upon that diagnosis a burden of certitude which, in its fallible nature, it cannot bear:

> No physician can predict with certainty how long any individual will live. Occasionally there are recoveries that seem miraculous, but they *do* happen. Shall we preclude all possibility of such occurrences by deliberately terminating a life? And even if we are urged to do so by a grief-stricken family, are we to be influenced by a decision made at a time of emotional upset which later may become a burden of guilt too great to be borne? Someone at such a time must remain a rock of strength and sober judgment. If not the physician, then who?[7]

Moreover, every diagnosis of incurability is subject to modification and reversal by the advances of science. It is true that the painfully and incurably ill patient will not enthuse over the prospect that science will find a cure for his disease in the long run. He knows too well that in the long run we shall all be dead. Yet how does he know for certain that the cure will not be found in the short run so that even his own life might be saved? To a considerable degree, medical progress is unpredictable. Even the bare prospect that a cure might soon be found should lead us to scrutinize the patient's death request more critically. The ever present, though bare, possibility of a cure should preclude euthanasia except where death would occur in the normal course in a brief matter of hours or days. Such immediate cases, however, involve all the general objections to euthanasia and the imminence of natural death would generally operate to impair the suffering or drugged patient's capacity to make a reasoned and reliable choice to die.

The allowance of voluntary euthanasia would clearly undermine the doctor-patient relation. It would alter the single-minded commitment to recovery that is the touchstone of the medical profession. The Hippocratic Oath includes a pledge that: "I will . . . abstain from whatever is deleterious and mischievous. I will give no deadly medicine to any one if asked, nor suggest any such counsel."[8] As one doctor put it:

> "The preservation of human life is not only the primary but the all-encompassing general law underlying the code of the physician. The advocation of exceptions to this law, no matter how humanitarian the motive of the advocate, cannot help but weaken it. . . . Do not ask life's guardian to be also its executioner. Do not turn medicine into a profession which could be practiced only by a psychopathic dual personality."[9]

A general sanction of euthanasia can also play havoc within families. In 1958, Otto Werner, aged sixty-nine, killed his sixty-three-year-old wife, Anna, by stuffing her mouth with rags. For two years she had suffered from severe arthritis and he had been "devoted and attentive" to his bedridden wife. But when they were told they were being sent "to an old people's home," he killed her and unsuccessfully tried to kill himself with sleeping pills. Mr. Werner pleaded guilty of manslaughter. Then, in an unprecedented ruling, Chief Justice A. L. Marovitz of the Criminal Court of Cook County, Illinois, induced him to change his plea to not guilty, whereupon the Chief Justice found him not guilty and released him so that he could go "home to his daughter and son without the stigma of a finding of guilty . . . and live out the rest of your life in as much peace as you can find it in your heart to have."[10] We certainly ought not to disparage the humanitarian motives of Chief Justice Marovitz. He was compassionate, as were the son and daughter of the defendant who asked to have him released to their custody. Nor should we castigate the distraught husband who slew his wife. It was involuntary euthanasia, but his immediate effort at suicide indicates the act was not motivated by a selfish desire to rid himself of a burden. But we are entitled to take a longer view. What does this do for the peace of mind of other aged incurables, bedridden and a burden on their long-suffering families? What, indeed, of the defendant himself? He might be pardoned a certain nervousness were he later to learn that he himself had contracted rheumatoid arthritis. It seems plain that in family and doctor-patient relations, if nowhere else, we should be absolutely assured that, no matter how irascible, helpless, or incontinent we become, we will not be legally executed for it.

The conclusive utilitarian argument against voluntary euthanasia of any sort is the irreducible possibility of error. Whether through a misdiagnosis of incurability or an erroneous evaluation of a patient's purpose and state of mind, the practice of voluntary euthanasia entails the enduring risk that some will be killed when they are not incurably ill or have not firmly consented. And a mistake here is irrevocable. Even if we approve mercy killing in principle, this utilitarian objection would be insurmountable. For in this matter of life and death we cannot tolerate any margin of error. Unlike compulsory military service, in which social need justifies the risk of innocent life, there is no comparable need here. And, unlike capital punishment, euthanasia involves the death of a certainly innocent person. When we impose the death penalty we do so only after it has been proven, beyond all reasonable doubt in elaborate judicial proceedings conducted pursuant to constitutional standards, that the defendant has committed a capital crime, usually the murder of an innocent victim. Capital punishment is justified, at least in theory, by the need to save innocent lives by deterring homicides. But there is no such justification for euthanasia. The supposed advantage is simply not worth the sacrifice.

Voluntary euthanasia is advocated ostensibly for the sole benefit of the patient. It is fair to say, however, that one purpose of voluntary euthanasia is to make things easier for the surviving relatives rather than for the lingering patient. Even if we accept the basic idea of mercy killing, the mere avoidance of inconvenience, however great, to the family or others, ought not to justify the risk of killing an unwilling or mistaken victim. Indeed, this factor of relief for the family causes the voluntary euthanasia proposals to verge into the involuntary variety.

There is reason to believe that a legalization of voluntary euthanasia would be a foot in the door for the involuntary sort. Indeed, compulsory euthanasia may be the ultimate aim of some leading advocates of voluntary mercy killing. When Lord Chorley spoke for a voluntary euthanasia bill in the House of Lords in 1950, he indicated that he considered it merely an interim measure:

> Another objection is that the Bill does not go far enough, because it applies only to adults and does not apply to children who come into the world deaf, dumb and crippled, and who have a much better cause than those for whom the Bill provides. That may be so, but we must go step by step.[11]

Other examples could be cited. One reason why voluntary programs of euthanasia tend to degenerate into compulsion is that even the voluntary type breeds a contempt for life. Glanville Williams advocates voluntary euthanasia for aged persons because medical science, in prolonging life expectancies, is "increasing the numbers of the aged and senile" beyond the point where we can adequately provide them "with better homes, domestic help, better hospital services and so on." He continues:

> Thus we still need to consider the help that could be given by a different solution, requiring not a social reorganization but a change in our philosophical attitudes. We should, in short, try to shake off the neurotic attitude towards death that has afflicted us for so long, and replace it with a realistic appreciation of death's biological function. To quote Dr. Slater again, "death plays a wholly favorable, indeed an essential, part in human economy. Without natural death, human societies and the human race itself would certainly be unable to thrive." Perhaps when we realize this, we may come to realize at the same time that there is a point in the degeneration of our bodies when life loses its value, and we may then be prepared voluntarily to leave the scene to our successors.[12]

If the social need to reduce the aged population is as great as Professor Williams makes it out to be, why should we condition the fulfillment of that need upon voluntary and spontaneous decisions by the old folks to liquidate themselves? It would seem appropriate to persuade them. And if, in their senility, they are so obdurate as not to respond to persuasion, why should they be preserved beyond the point "when life loses its value"?

Voluntary euthanasia can be justified only on the basic assumptions that there is such a thing as a life not worth living, that suffering has no meaning, and that the utility of a life is to be judged only by material considerations without reference to any spiritual standards. If the worth of a life is to be judged only by whether it is temporally useful or satisfying, and it is to be preserved only so far, there is no reason in principle why the decision as to its continuance cannot be made by someone other than the possessor of that life. Through military conscription, persons in authority can require an innocent person to risk his life for the defense of the state. In capital punishment, the competent authorities can directly kill a person who has forfeited his right to life by committing a proportionately serious crime. These are based on the assumption that conscription and capital punishment are sufficiently necessary to save other lives and to preserve law and order. But once we authorize voluntary euthanasia, we affirm that the "willing" victim's life is pointless and has no value. If we admit that his life has no value, how can we deny the right of the authorities to reach that decision by applying "objective criteria" regardless of the will of the victim? If the victim's own request is sufficient to warrant the termination of his life, for his own good, why should he be deprived of the opportunity of a "merciful release" merely because he is an infant, insane, or too obtuse to realize the worthlessness of his own life? Enter thus involuntary euthanasia "for his own good." Once we admit involuntary euthanasia for the good of the victim, it is a short step to employing it for the good of the state.

An acceptance of the basic error that there is such a thing as a life not worth living can only end in involuntary elimination of the worthless ones. Once the basic fallacy is adopted, the tendency is to slide into involuntary elimination of the aged, the helpless, and finally the socially or politically undesirable. The lesson of Nazi Germany is indelibly clear on the point. The mass exterminations there began with the "merciful" killing of those with incurable physical or mental illness.

Hannah Arendt notes that the final solution to the Jewish Problem "was not carried out by shooting, hence through violence, but in the gas factories, which, from beginning to end, were closely connected with the "euthanasia program" ordered by Hitler in the first weeks of the war and applied to the mentally sick in Germany up to the invasion of Russia."[13] It is obviously not fair, on the one hand, to suggest that all advocates of euthanasia are latent Nazis. On the other hand, it is reasonable to conclude that a measure so drastic and antithetical to the sanctity of innocent life carries within itself the seeds of abuse and potential subordination to political ends. No episode in history has served to dramatize the danger of political control over innocent life more than the cosmic disaster that befell the victims of Nazi Germany. The great interest of humanity in avoiding a similar recurrence dictates that proposals relating to the right to life be closely scrutinized for kinship to the theories underlying the German experience.

A letter from Hitler, dated September 1, 1939, provided the documentary impetus for the euthanasia program:

> Reichsleiter Boukler and Dr. Brandt, M.D., are charged with the responsibility of enlarging the authority of certain physicians to be designated by name in such a manner that persons who, according to human judgment, are incurable can, upon a most careful diagnosis of their condition of sickness, be accorded a mercy death.[14]

This Hitler decree was not itself an order and no law or formal order was ever promulgated to authorize the involuntary euthanasia program that had long been planned by psychiatrists and officials.[15] Hitler had advocated euthanasia in *Mein Kampf*.[16] The book, *The Release of the Destruction of Life Devoid of Value*, written in 1920 by the law professor Karl Binding and the psychiatrist Alfred Hoche, effectively conditioned the German doctors and people to accept the idea of euthanasia, even before the Nazi era.

The euthanasia program began in late 1939.[17] In its early stages the notion was cultivated that the program was for the benefit of the victims. A typical form letter sent to relatives of mental patients killed under the program touched on this theme:

> Because of her grave mental illness life was a torment for the deceased. You must therefore look on her death as a release.[18]

Contrary to popular assumption, Jews were excluded from the early stages of the involuntary euthanasia program in Germany. Dr. Fredric Wertham described this curious development:

> During the first phase of the program, Jewish mental patients, old and young,

were strictly spared and excluded. The reason given was that they did not deserve the "benefit" of psychiatric euthanasia. This lasted up to the second half of 1940. Eventually they were all rounded up, however, and by 1941, practically without exception, were exterminated.[19]

Jews were excluded because they were not worthy, but, quite inconsistently, German veterans of the First World War were also excluded, presumably because they did not deserve such a fate.[20]

Involuntary euthanasia is open to several objections from a utilitarian view. One is the elasticity of the word "illness." It can hardly be restricted to cancer, or even physical illness. If it is extended to other physical ailments or to mental illness, where on earth shall it stop? The only restraint on the indefinite extension of the proscribed class will be the self-restraint of the officials whom we endow with the power to dispose. One observer commented on this extension of the Nazi program:

> . . . The beginnings at first were merely a subtle shift in emphasis in the basic attitude of the physicians. *It started with the acceptance of the attitude, basic in the euthanasia movement, that there is such a thing as life not worthy to be lived.* This attitude in its early stages concerned itself merely with the severely and chronically sick. Gradually the sphere of those to be included in this category was enlarged to encompass the socially unproductive, the ideologically unwanted, the racially unwanted and finally all non-Germans. But it is important to realize that the infinitely small wedged-in lever from which this entire trend of mind received its impetus was the attitude toward the non-rehabilitatable sick.[21]

We cannot rest on the comforting assumption that the Nazi engineers of extermination were a super-breed of monsters. On the contrary, they were generally ordinary people, meticulous functionaries, who could be gentle and kind in their private lives but relentless in performing their duty. The more arrogant ones were convinced they were acting for the good of mankind. When it was suggested to one SS general that the bodies should be burned instead of buried, to prevent discovery, because "a future generation might think differently of these matters," he replied:

> "But, gentlemen, if after us such a cowardly and rotten generation should arise that it does not understand our work which is so good and so necessary, then, gentlemen, all National Socialism will have been for nothing. On the contrary, bronze plaques should be put up with the inscription that it was we, we who had the courage to achieve this gigantic task."[22]

It is relevant, too, that the mercy-killing program was carried out arbitrarily and with considerable cruelty. There were no real examinations to determine who should be selected for the program. The decisive factor was not the degree of insanity or illness but rather the usefulness for work.[23]

"Hitler's ultimate reason for the establishment of the Euthanasia Program in Germany was to eliminate those people confined to insane asylums and similar institutions who could no longer be of any use to the Reich. They were considered useless objects and Hitler felt that by exterminating these so-called useless eaters, it would be possible to relieve more doctors, male and female nurses, and other personnel, hospital beds and other facilities for the armed forces."[24]

Many selected for the program were subjected to medical experiments, including freezing, malaria tests, mustard gas, and starvation diet experiments. "Useless eaters" were deliberately and literally starved to death.[25] The Reich Committee for Research on Hereditary and Constitutional Diseases conducted "the killing of mentally and bodily deficient children."[26] At Belcec the naked victims were lured into a gas chamber with a Star of David on the roof. An SS man shouted to the people, "Nothing whatever will happen to you. All you have to do is to breathe deeply; it strengthens the lungs. This inhalation is a necessary measure against contagious diseases; it is a very good disinfectant!" The building bore a sign, "Heckenholt Foundation." Heckenholt was the SS man in charge of the diesel engine that pumped gas into the room where the victims were packed like sardines. Later the doors were opened and the bodies removed, most to be buried or burned, and some to be used for soap. "The dead were still standing like stone statues, there having been no room for them to fall or bend over. Though dead, the families could still be recognized, their hands still clasped."[27] As Thomas Merton said, "Auschwitz was a family camp."[28]

One of the little ironies of history is the Nazi law passed on November 24, 1933, for the protection of animals. "This law states explicitly that it is designed to prevent cruelty and indifference of man towards animals and to awaken and develop sympathy and understanding for animals as one of the highest moral virtues. The soul of the German people should abhor the principle of mere utility without consideration of the moral aspects."[29] If this principle had been applied to humans, euthanasia and Nuremberg never would have occurred.

The euthanasia program was formally ended in the summer of 1941, when the rumors of missing relatives at home created a morale crisis in the military service. Morale problems had also been created by the practice of euthanatizing soldiers with serious head wounds. However, although the large-scale gassing stopped then, the "mercy killings" continued until the end of the war in 1945.[30]

Proponents of euthanasia today often say that it is a purely medical matter beyond the province of the law. The doctor-patient relation is viewed as sacrosanct and in this relation the doctor naturally gravitates into the leading role. The Nazi experience taught us a great deal about the sanctity of life and the predictable abuse when innocent life is subjected to political ends. But it also taught us something about doctors. The euthanasia program owed its inception and execution to the doctors, and especially the psychiatrists.[31] The doctors had both the unfettered power to select and the duty to kill those selected. As one defendant at Nuremberg testified:

"All persons subjected to the Euthanasia Program did not have an opportunity to decide whether they wanted a mercy death, nor were their relatives contacted for approval or disapproval. The decision was purely within the discretion of the doctors. The program was not restricted to those cases in which the person was 'in extremis.' "[32]

Certainly a person should not forfeit the protection of the law when he comes under a doctor's care. Unfortunately some medical proponents of euthanasia, abortion, and kindred practices operate under the illusion that they are God. Their intellectual forbear was the doctor-defendant at Nuremberg who stated that he decided on a medical career because it would enable him to become "master over life and death."[33]

It is worth while to reflect upon the Nazi experience. But it would be an oversimplification to dismiss it as a German phenomenon. The Soviet liquidation of some 5 million kulaks—the landholding peasants—between 1928 and 1933 was an act of euthanasia in the broad sense. The kulaks were considered useless obstacles to the achievement of collectivized agriculture. They shared the fate of the "useless eaters" of Nazi Germany.[34] The Communist Chinese effort to liquidate the Tibetans as a people is similar. Nor are Americans immune to the tendency to disparage the value of life. At the end of World War II, the Morgenthau Plan envisioned turning millions of Germans over to Moscow as slave labor. Harry Dexter White, the accused Communist spy who authored the Plan, said this was "merely a part of the reparations problem in the same way you want certain machines from Germany."[35] The common ground between involuntary euthanasia of a single patient in a hospital room and genocide is the assumption that some lives are not worth living. The difference is quantitative only.

The potential for political abuse should lead us to reject euthanasia even without the experience of our own generation. With that experience freshly in mind, it is nothing short of obscene to propose euthanasia today.

We have sketched up to this point some of the pragmatic fallacies in euthanasia of either the voluntary or compulsory type. However, there are deeper objections to those proposals.

The theme of this book is the need for vindication of the sanctity of innocent life. The euthanasia issue is only one of several, but it measures our success in restoring respect for life. To the extent that "mercy killing" is seriously advanced and favored, it measures our failure to generate a popular dedication to the right to life in all its implications.

More precisely, the drive to legalize euthanasia reflects the overall flight from personal accountability and responsibility for others. The proponents of involuntary euthanasia are hardly championing the rights of others in any coherent sense. Essentially their position is selfish and a flight from responsibility for those who are less fortunate or of whom they disapprove. Involuntary euthanasia, one is entitled to suspect, is often conceived as a device for the benefit not of the victim but of his relatives, the doctors, and the social engineers who decide which lives are worthless to the state. The same suspicions are warranted, in a different way, with respect to the campaign to legalize voluntary euthanasia.

It is increasingly clear that euthanasia is the logical end of the current agitation for abortion. More precisely, a coherent defense against euthanasia requires a strong offensive against abortion. Both of these subordinate the right to live to the lesser needs of others or to the social design of the state. If the validity of either be acknowl-

edged, our objections to Auschwitz and Buchenwald will be reduced
to the functional and the sentimental:

> Resist beginnings. All too late the cure,
> When ills have gathered strength by long delay.

It is not enough, however, merely to affirm the sanctity of life.
A successful offensive against these evil trends must affirm as well
the importance of personal accountability and responsibility, not
only to ourselves and our fellow men, but to God. Unless we stand
on a foundation of the spirit, our only objection to euthanasia can
be pragmatic, and therefore subject to being outweighed in a particular case of great need and unusual circumstances. A reliance
solely on functional arguments itself disparages respect for life, since
it implicitly concedes that if the mechanical difficulties could be sur-
mounted in a particular case, euthanasia would be tolerable. In truth,
however, euthanasia of any sort is absolutely intolerable and it must
be considered so even if all the utilitarian objections were fully answered. For euthanasia basically disrupts the relation between man
and God and between man and his fellow man. Under any colora-
tion, it is an exercise in presumption and self-concern. The only way
to restore personal accountability and responsibility for others is to
condemn euthanasia without reservation. Its advocates ought to be
rejected with the finality reserved for those who would play God
with the human race.

It is prudent and urgent to resist even the slightest suggestion
of euthanasia. Our opposition, however, should not be so misdi-
rected that we fail to make the distinctions required by sound medical practice and respect for life. To say that the doctor's duty is to
preserve life and not to destroy it does not mean that the barest
flicker of life must be preserved indefinitely at all costs and through
the use of extraordinary means. There is a point at which medical
efforts are unavailing and the doctor may properly let the patient die
in peace without resorting to bizarre and predictably fruitless measures. The Victorian poet A. H. Clough described the doctor's obligation in his "Modern Decalogue":

> Thou shalt not kill, yet need not strive
> Officiously to keep alive.[36]

67

While a doctor's primary task is to save his patient's life, the distinction between ordinary and extraordinary means is applicable here. There is an absolute obligation on the doctor to use all ordinary and available means to preserve life, but there is no absolute obligation to use means that are extraordinary. A course of treatment would be extraordinary in this sense if, for example, it involved excessive pain or an expense that would reduce the patient's family to penury without offering any significant hope of saving the patient's life. This principle was amplified by Pope Pius XII in an address to an audience of physicians in 1957.[37]

What is extraordinary will depend upon the facts of the particular case and largely upon the judgment of the attending physician. However, the duty to use all available ordinary means cannot be evaded. The optional character of extraordinary means cannot be used to mask a practice of "negative euthanasia" through withholding measures that are properly considered ordinary. At Neasden Hospital in London a notice to doctors and ward sisters in 1966 directed that in cases of cardiac arrest patients in certain categories—those over sixty-five and those with malignant diseases or chronic chest or kidney diseases—were not to be resuscitated. Those patients were to have their medical treatment cards labeled "NTBR—Not To Be Resuscitated." When a public furor resulted, the Ministry of Health forbade all hospitals in the country to impose any automatic ban on resuscitation:

> No patient should be excluded from consideration for resuscitation by reason of age or diagnostic classification alone, and without regard to all the individual circumstances.
> Any form of general instruction is wholly unacceptable.[38]

During the months that the notice was on the board, it appeared that no patient who might have benefited from resuscitation efforts failed to receive them. Nevertheless, the idea created considerable shock. And sick humor, too: a cartoon in the London *Evening Standard* showed one elderly man in a wheel chair asking another: "Is this one of those hospitals where one daren't stop breathing?"[39] When medical bureaucrats attempt to standardize the limits of their life-saving function, the result is cold-blooded and less than human.

While we reject the notion that murder is an acceptable alternative to suffering, it would be unsound to infer that suffering is a positive good in itself. A proper respect for life is not at all inconsistent with the use of pain-killing drugs. Pope Pius XII took a middle ground on this issue in a 1957 address to an audience of anesthetists. He noted that:

". . . the growth in the love of God and in abandonment to His will does not come from the sufferings themselves which are accepted, but from the intention in the will, supported by grace. This intention, in many of the dying, can be strengthened and become more active if their sufferings are eased, for these sufferings increase the state of weakness and physical exhaustion, check the ardor of soul and sap the moral powers instead of sustaining them. On the other hand, the suppression of pain removes any tension in body and mind, renders prayer easy, and makes possible a more generous gift of self. If some dying persons accept their suffering as a means of expiation and a source of merits in order to go forward in the love of God and in abandonment to His will, do not force anesthetics on them. They should rather be aided to follow their own way. Where the situation is entirely different, it would be inadvisable to suggest to dying persons the ascetical considerations set out above, and it is to be remembered that instead of assisting towards expiation and merit, suffering can also furnish occasion for new faults."[40]

Medical science has progressed so rapidly that doctors are increasingly called upon to decide which of several patients they will save. When only one kidney machine is available, doctors must decide whether it will go to save the life of the young child, the thirty-year-old factory worker with a wife and three children, or the grandmother whose husband is dead and all of whose children are grown. A similar problem is presented by the transplanting of hearts, kidneys, and other vital organs. Every year eight thousand Americans die because there are not enough kidneys or kidney machines.[41] The doctor's decision in a case of this sort is not comparable to a decision to euthanatize. For when a doctor decides to perform the transplant on one of two patients, where the medical chances of success are comparable in both, he makes no affirmative decision to kill the patient upon whom he does not operate. Rather he strives to use the available resources to save life and if those resources—whether transplanted hearts or kidney machines—are insufficient to save all the lives that need saving, that deficiency cannot be charged to the doctor. The situation does involve the doctor in an awful dilemma, where he has to make a nearly Godlike judgment. But the decision has to be made and, given the limited availability of the novel life-saving method, he cannot escape it.

A more delicate question is posed by the new heart-transplant technique. In the first heart transplant, the donor of the heart was clinically or medically dead, in that her spontaneous respiration and circulation had ceased. She was given artificial respiration while the recipient was prepared for the transplant and the preparations for the removal of her heart were made. Then her heart was removed and the artificial respirator was turned off. When did she die, before or after her heart was removed and the respirator turned off? From the earliest times, the moment of death has been commonly recognized as the moment when the heart stops beating. It may now be possible to establish the moment as "brain death," through the use of an electroencephalogram, so that the patient would be determined to be irreversibly dead even though the heart and lungs are kept functioning by an artificial device.[42] Actually, no new juridical questions are posed here. Rather it is a question of the moral and scientific determination of the moment of death. Once the donor is conclusively determined to be dead, according to the relevant scientific criteria, his heart can be removed for the transplant. If the heart is removed before he dies, then, because removal of the heart causes death, we have a case of euthanasia for the benefit of the donee.

It would seem clear, also, that an organ transplant ought not to be performed without the consent of the donor or his surviving kin. Even when the surviving kin consent, it ought not to be done if the deceased donor expressly forbade it. The body does not belong to the state and the state can hardly consign it to a spare parts pool, contrary to the expressed desire of the deceased, without disparaging the personal responsibility one has for his own body and his life.

Opposition to euthanasia is not inconsistent with approval of reasonable and proper medical experiments. A serious question, however, is presented by experiments conducted on patients without their consent. We oppose euthanasia, particularly of the compulsory sort, because it subordinates the person's very right to life to such utilitarian concerns as may motivate the euthanasor. Unauthorized medical experiments may not result in the termination of life itself but they do involve an invasion of the personal right to bodily integrity and self-determination.

One recent experiment in the United States was performed on eighteen children about to undergo heart surgery for congenital heart disease. The experiment concerned the unrelated problem of the effect of the thymus gland on skin grafts. During their heart operations, all eighteen children had skin grafts sutured to their chest walls. Eleven of them also had their thymuses removed, while the seven others did not and were used as a control group. The eleven children were thus subjected to removal of the thymus—an operation with unpredictable long-term effects—in order to study the fairly uncommon and wholly unrelated problem of skin transplants.[43] Neither the children nor their parents were informed of the experiment, let alone asked for permission.

In 1964, twenty-two elderly, seriously ill patients at the Jewish Chronic Disease Hospital in Brooklyn were injected with live cancer cells as part of a research program to determine the capacity of debilitated bodies to reject cancer cells. In fact, the experiment involved no danger that the patients would contract cancer from it. However, they were not informed that the injection was of cancer cells or that the experiment was not for their own benefit. The doctors who conducted the experiment were later reprimanded for it by the State Board of Regents.[44]

One common factor in these two cases was that the experiments were unrelated to the ailments of the patients. There is something frightening about doctors using their patients as unwitting guinea pigs for experiments unrelated to their own welfare. On the other hand, it would be unrealistic to draw an artificially sharp line forbidding all such tests. Medical and pharmacological progress obviously depends upon adequate testing of new procedures and drugs. It is fair to say, however, that no patient should be used for unrelated experiments without his consent. That consent, moreover, should be asked only after full disclosure of the relevant facts and attendant risks. The experiment, too, should be of sufficient importance to justify the risk and inconvenience to the patient. These criteria were generally embodied in the Nuremberg rules that evolved from the trials of the German doctors,[45] the Helsinki Declaration adopted by the World Medical Association in 1964, and the Ethical

Guidelines for Clinical Investigation issued by the American Medical Association in 1966.[46] It is questionable, however, whether the general statement of principles answers all the difficult questions that arise in practice. Some relaxation of the requirement of full disclosure might be justified in some blind or double-blind experiments that are sufficiently important, involve no significant risk to the patient, and would be frustrated by the patient's awareness of the fact and nature of the experiment.[47] The problem, moreover, is not capable of resolution through a simple prohibition in the criminal law. It involves issues of professional judgment, permissible research, frankness in the doctor-patient relation, and similar factors more capable of solution by professional and licensing agencies. But a narrowly drawn criminal statute could serve a limited purpose of defining the public policy unequivocally, while reserving the sanctions for flagrant and willful cases.

The attending physician, of course, has to have greater latitude in conducting experiments on his patient to determine the best treatment for that patient himself. The doctor here must be governed by a single-minded purpose to benefit his patient and a prudent sense of proportion as to the means employed. It is not in this area, however, that the analogy to euthanasia is found. Rather that problem arises where experiments unrelated to the patient's welfare are conducted, that is, where he is used as a means to benefit future patients or to achieve some social objective. Although the harm to the unwitting subject of the experiments is not lethal, the invasion of his privacy, of his right to be left alone, is as real in principle as when his life is snuffed out by the euthanasor. In both cases, the safeguard against abuse will be found primarily in a self-restraint founded on a respect for human life and the human person. The law can and should reinforce these attitudes where practicable but it cannot substitute for them over the long run.

5

SUICIDE

It was a fog-shrouded Sunday, February 11, 1968, when a navy jet trainer smashed into the San Francisco–Oakland Bay Bridge, raining flaming debris onto cars and trucks before plunging into the bay with its two-man crew. Traffic on the bridge was closed for three hours. After two hours of the delay, one waiting motorist, John Canfield Morgan, a twenty-year-old Stanford University student, got out of his car, ran to the bridge railing, climbed over it, and jumped to his death in the water below. One witness said it happened so quickly that no one had a chance to prevent him from leaping.[1]

John Morgan evidently was one of some 20,000 suicides in the United States each year. There are also at least nine or ten times as many attempts as there are completed suicides. Every twenty-five minutes a person in this country kills himself. Suicide today is fairly routine. It is the tenth leading cause of death in the United States. In the United States in 1966, 20,160 persons took their own lives. This is a rate of 10.3 per 100,000 population.[2] This rate is fairly constant in the United States, although it varied from 14.1 to 17.4 in the depression years of the 1930s.[3] Dr. Edwin S. Shneidman, chief of the Center for Studies of Suicide Prevention of the National Institute of Mental Health, says the official estimates are grossly understated and that the true figures may be two or three times higher.[4] Suicide is the second leading cause of death among American college students and the third among persons aged fifteen to nineteen.[5] Generally, three times as many men as women commit suicide.[6] The suicide rate in this country is higher in the more affluent sections of the economy and is more than twice as high among whites as among Negroes.[7] "In today's culture—so competitive, so complex, so frightening—there seems to be a built-in minimum suicide rate. And its shadow extends farther than we ever realized.

73

Psychologists tell us that there are millions of hidden suicides every year: the alcoholics, the accident-prone, the person who neglects himself and his welfare until he wins eventual death by default."[8]

The World Health Organization reported in 1966 that the highest rate for suicides was in Hungary, with 28.6 per 100,000 population for the year 1964. Austria was next with 22.8, followed by Denmark with 21.0. Sweden had a rate of 19.8, which means 1514 persons committed suicide in that country in 1964. The lowest suicide rates among nations of substantial size were in Ireland, with 2.5, and Spain, with 2.6. Mexico had a low rate of 1.9.

It would be easy to multiply statistics in this area. But, beyond establishing that suicide is a substantial problem, figures are dubious because they reflect only reported occurrences. An undeterminable number of suicides is not reported as such. In considering attempted suicides, the ratio of the unreported has to be even higher than for successful ones. In any event, most suicide attempts are really appeals for help and the total number of reported suicides must include some "accidental" ones that were never intended by the self-victim to go really that far.

The word "suicide" means to kill oneself. Suicide is a form of voluntary euthanasia, except that the one who kills himself was not otherwise in danger of death. It is defined more precisely as "where a man of discretion and *compos mentis*, voluntarily kills himself by stabbing, poison, or any other way."[9]

It is urged by some, including the Swedish economist, Gunnar Myrdal, that suicide is a purely private matter. Myrdal described the Swedish attitude on suicide:

> In England, for example, suicide is still a crime. In most countries, particularly the Catholic ones, it is a grave sin against the Creator. In secularized Sweden, it is not a crime and not a sin, though a regrettable deviation from normal behavior. When committed with a sane mind, it is gradually becoming viewed, however, as almost a human right and a civil liberty. In any case, it is a strictly personal and family matter.[10]

If we concede that each person has a right to end his own life, we infer that some lives are simply not worth living to the completion of their normal term. Suicide is different from killing in self-defense, capital punishment, and war, since all of those involve the involuntary death of one whose right to life is forfeited by his own

74

action or as an incident to a just war. Suicide, like voluntary euthanasia, is self-chosen. The arguments to condone suicide are subject
to the same weaknesses as those to excuse voluntary euthanasia,
excepting the factor of mental capacity. The person contemplating
suicide, in relative physical ease and free from the pain of terminal
illness, is obviously in a better position to make a rational decision
than is the pain-racked patient who pleads in his desperation for a
merciful release. The would-be suicide's right to decide to kill himself cannot be denied on the ground that the circumstances make
that decision inherently unreliable. Therefore, suicide presents us
squarely with the issue of whether, with full understanding and
clarity of purpose, one has the right to end his own life. Suicide also
merits treatment apart from euthanasia, because it is a substantial
problem in its own dimensions.

Suicide was punishable at English common law by forfeiture of
the suicide's land and goods, unless he was insane at the time of the
act. The practice of forfeiture, which was recognized as early as
A.D. 967, eventually led to the formalization of suicide as a felony,
since forfeiture of land and goods to the Crown was one of the usual
penalties for a felony. The suicide's body was buried ignominiously
at a crossroads or on a highway, with a stake driven through the body
or a stone placed over the face. These were intended to prevent the
body from rising in ghostly form. The last incident of crossroads
burial in England occurred in 1823 and that same year a statute
abolished the practice.

Suicide is no longer a crime in England and there is no legal
prohibition against church burial, although the Church of England
still bars a ritual funeral unless the suicide was mentally unbalanced.

The English punishment of suicide as a crime was not widely
adopted in the United States. A Massachusetts statute of 1660 forbade Christian burial for suicides and declared that they "shall be
buried in some common highway" and "a cartload of stones laid
upon the grave, as a brand of infamy, and as a warning to others to
beware of the like damnable practices."[11] The statute was not copied
in other states and eventually was repealed in 1823. In at least forty-
one American states suicide is not in any way a crime. In New York
and a few other states, suicide is considered a "grave public wrong"
although it is not a crime.[12]

In England it is a felony to attempt suicide or to aid or persuade another to do so. In most American states attempted suicide is not a crime, but in the majority of states aiding and abetting a suicide is a crime. If a person who is attempting suicide accidentally kills another in the process, he may be prosecuted for murder or manslaughter in England and in most American states.[13]

It is difficult to frame a coherent policy on suicide. We begin with the fact that a successful perpetrator is beyond the reach of the law. We surely ought not to forfeit the property of the deceased. Forfeiture worked a hardship only on the surviving family and it would be of dubious utility in discouraging suicides today.

But in a more fundamental way suicide cannot be regarded as simply a matter for the criminal law. Each case involves a special calculus of despair, with insanity as a disturbingly frequent factor. Why, it is said, would a sane man willfully destroy himself? And, to be sure, the issue of mental imbalance must be considered in each case. Our proper tendency is to give the benefit of the doubt to insanity, to infer that the victim was not himself when he took the poison or pulled the trigger, rather than to defame his memory by concluding that he did such a thing with a clear head and deliberately. But we ought to beware the generalization that all suicides are mentally unbalanced. As one authority put it, "Studies of hundreds of genuine suicide notes indicate that although the suicidal person is extremely unhappy, he is not necessarily mentally ill."[14] It is an oversimplification to conclude that suicide is necessarily or even presumptively due to mental imbalance. Rather the causes of suicide are still widely debated and conjectured. Emile Durkheim, in his leading work on suicide in 1897,[15] attributed suicide to the social conditions attendant upon urbanization and industrialization. Recent studies have emphasized the isolation of persons living alone in the cities, the rootless mobility of modern life, and the breakdown of the family as leading causes of suicide. Freud, on the other hand, attributed suicide psychiatrically to an explosion of aggressive guilt feelings within the suicide himself. At least one study has found a deadening of religious faith to be a factor in suicides and attempted suicides in Sweden.[16]

It would be interesting to canvass in detail the various theories on the causation of suicide. And any policy to deal effectively with suicide should seek to minimize the social, economic, psychological, and spiritual conditions that contribute to the problem. However, before we can frame a policy on suicide, we must first determine whether suicide is wrong. There are those today as in every age who say that suicide is a natural right or at least that it is justified in certain circumstances. On the contrary, suicide, in the sense of a deliberate and direct killing of oneself, is always wrong. In the words of G. K. Chesterton, "Not only is suicide a sin, it is *the* sin. It is the ultimate and absolute evil . . . the man who kills himself, kills all men . . . he wipes out the world."[17]

Suicide is wrong, not because it is messy or inconvenient but, for one thing, because it is a willful contradiction of the deep-seated natural urge to self-preservation. It is contrary to nature and it violates the self-love a man ought properly to have for himself. Moreover, suicide deprives society of the presence and service the community is entitled to expect even from the most wretched of its members. These two reasons were advanced by Thomas Aquinas. Aristotle emphasized the second and further denounced suicide as an act of cowardice:

> Yet to kill oneself as a means of escape from poverty or disappointed love or bodily or mental anguish is the deed of a coward rather than a brave man. To run away from trouble is a form of cowardice and, while it is true that the suicide braves death, he does it not for some noble object but to escape some ill.[18]

These two reasons, depending upon the natural instinct of self-preservation and the assumed duty to the community, are essentially secular. Involving no supernatural factor, they presumably could be outweighed by compelling factors indicating suicide to be the best thing for the individual and the community in a particular case. Why may not the captured spy swallow poison when faced with torture that will cause him to reveal vital secrets? A pragmatic calculation could find suicide defensible and even laudable in such a case. Indeed, even some Catholic theologians would support suicide by a spy acting under orders to take his own life. Redemptorist Father Bernard Häring believes the spy would not be "arbitrarily and independently" taking his own life and therefore would not be committing suicide within the meaning of the Church's prohibition. A fellow Redemptorist, the late Father Francis J. Connell, former dean of the School of Sacred Theology at Catholic University, disagreed. Direct self-destruction of an innocent person, said Father Connell, "is always a moral evil." He continued:

> It has been the constant teaching of the Catholic Church that the state has no direct authority over the life of an innocent person. Furthermore, an innocent person has no authorization from God to kill himself directly.
>
> An aviator in war may dive into the enemy's warship with the direct purpose of damaging the ship, although his death follows indirectly. But in the case of the spy, death is inflicted directly, and the good effect—the preservation of important secrets—follows from the death of the spy. In other words, we have a case of a bad means to a good end.[19]

The point here is not to provide guidance for prospective spies. The suicidal spy, however, is symbolic. His case, and other extreme examples, show that only a supernatural foundation will support a principled and unyielding opposition to suicide. Father Häring, who sustains the spy's right to kill himself, and Father Connell, who rejects it, both argue from a supernatural premise that suicide is an offense to God. They differ over interpreting the terms of the divine prohibition. But even though one theologian supports the suicide in the particular case, it is important that Father Connell could not have opposed it except on a spiritual, supernatural plane. This divine prohibition is the third and the only unyielding reason why suicide is wrong. Thomas Aquinas insisted that, since God alone has control over life and death, suicide is a usurpation of God's power. Blackstone echoed this view:

> And also the law of England wisely and religiously considers, that no man hath a power to destroy life, but by commission from God, the author of it: and as the suicide is guilty of a double offense: one spiritual, in invading the prerogative of the Almighty, and rushing into his immediate presence uncalled for; the other temporal, against the king, who hath an interest in the preservation of all his subjects; the law has therefore ranked this among the highest crimes, making it a peculiar species of felony committed on one's self.[20]

This book is not a theological treatise. Nor does it purport to offer a guide for the spiritual life. It does, however, argue for a renewed reverence toward life. Although respect for life is hardly the exclusive property of theists, their ultimate foundation gives their position a coherence lacking in merely humanitarian approaches.

Suicide is an issue on which a renewal of reverence for life would have an important bearing. It is hardly likely that, in a society that treasures the sanctity of life, the act of suicide could ever be viewed as an acceptable and neutral matter of personal choice. It is wholly inconceivable that suicide could be so regarded in a society that premises its regard for life on the conviction that God is its Author and Disposer. Conversely, and more to the point, the growth of a casual attitude toward suicide can influence a society's entire attitude toward the right to life. It can also betray a general cheapening of life, without which the spread of euthanasia, abortion, and other corrosive practices would be simply impossible.

Suicide is always wrong because in fact there is a God of Providence Who has created us out of nothing and Whose prerogative we would deny by "rushing into His immediate presence uncalled for." It is not surprising that in our secularized society suicide has become more common and less horrifying. For of all the issues treated in this book, suicide raises the ultimate spiritual question in an unalloyed and inescapable way. It is possible for one who believes in God to think that suicide in some cases is not a sin. But it is almost inevitable that one who denies or ignores God will think so. A study by Dr. Daniel De Sole of the Veterans Administration Hospital in Albany, New York, showed that 26% of all deaths among physicians aged twenty-five to thirty-nine years of age were suicides. The rate for all white males in that age group is 9%. Interestingly, the doctors with the highest suicide rate are the psychiatrists. The editors of *Triumph* offered a possible reason for this:

> The young doctors, it seems, suffer primarily from a lack of hope. Unsustained by the expectation of life hereafter, and unguided by divine plans for their lives here below, they seek fulfillment in the City of Man. The doctors, especially the psychiatrists, are called on to perform the role of shepherds of men.
>
> Doctors are the priests of secular liberal society. But for such a role as this, psychology and medicine together are entirely inadequate. They are much too superficial to plumb the depth of life and measure the meaning of man. For that the transcendental view of the real priest is indispensable. Thus the failure of these poor young men is inevitable; and their failure frustrates them. . . . To escape these disappointments, suicide presents the doctors, with their drug-filled cupboards and their empty souls, an easy way out.[21]

It is important to put suicide in its place as an act of irresponsibility to oneself, probably to others, and certainly to God. But it is no less important to deal compassionately with the person disposed to suicide than it is to condemn the practice in the law. There are a few broadly specific ways that these two objectives can be sought by a society bent upon promoting respect for life.

In the first place, it is senseless to make the act of suicide itself a crime. Punishment of the successful suicide would be impossible and we surely ought not to return to the barbarism of punishing his family by forfeiting his property. Even though not itself a crime, however, suicide should be regarded as a grave social wrong. One who deliberately aids a person in committing or attempting suicide should be punished for murder or at least manslaughter. This should be theoretically so, whether the aid was active, through handing poison to the prospective suicide, or passive, through willfully refusing to remove poison from the reach of the person who had proclaimed his purpose to use it. Passive complicity of the latter sort would rarely be capable of sufficient proof to convict. But it ought not to be minimized in principle on that account. Rather, a sound policy would severely punish all forms of abetting suicide, as far as it can be done within the framework of due process of law. To remove such punishment would encourage those who are inclined to dispose of wealthy relatives or others whose demise would be rewarding or convenient. Murder can be engineered to look like suicide. It would be easier to get away with it when the murderer could swear without fear of punishment, or contradiction by the deceased, that all he did was hand him the gun with which he shot himself.

Attempted suicide should be a crime. Otherwise, how could aiding and abetting an attempted or completed suicide logically be a crime? But attempted suicide should be criminal for a more basic reason. The deterrent effect of a criminal sanction could discourage a number of potential suicides from making the attempt, although it can fairly be answered that it would merely make them more careful about making a successful job of it. But most attempted suicides are not genuine attempts at all, only demonstrations and appeals for help.[22] A criminal penalty for attempting suicide might discourage some from staging such an appeal and it might save the lives of some who "attempt" suicide as an appeal for help and who unintentionally succeed in killing themselves. Although we should define attempted suicide as a crime, we ought not always to treat it as such. The attempted suicide is not always mentally incompetent or insane. But he is always in deep emotional trouble:

> Fortunately, no one is 100 per cent suicidal. Psychologists today realize that even the most ardent death wish is ambivalent. People cut their throats and plead to be saved at the same moment. Suicide notes often illustrate the fatal illogic of the suicidal person, the mixing of cross-purposed desires: "Dear Mary, I hate you. Love, John." "I'm tired. There must be something fine for you. Love, Bill." These simple, but pathetic messages are actual suicide notes. Like the iceberg's tip above the surface, they hint at the awesome mass below. When a man is suicidal, his perspective freezes. He wants to live, but can see no way. His logic is confused, but he cannot clear his head. He stumbles into death, still gasping for life, even in those last moments when he tries to write down how he feels.[23]

It should be the business of the law to help the person who has tried to take his own life. The definition of the attempt as a crime would give the courts a handle to establish their jurisdiction. But there should be a procedure similar to those in New York and California for narcotics addicts. If a suicide attempt is made, the courts should have the power, and should be encouraged, to drop the criminal charge, without even subjecting the defendant to a public appearance in court. The defendant should be required to undergo psychiatric and medical care, on an outpatient or institutional basis, where the court believes it would be in his best interest. The purpose of such a law could well be served if not one attempted suicide ever served a day in jail and if the court operated simply as a clearinghouse for needed treatment. But it would still be prudent to define attempted suicide as a punishable crime. For there might well be cases where psychiatric and medical care could do no conceivable good and where the defendant ought to be put away for a while for his own protection. It might be objected that a determined suicide who is beyond the reach of psychiatrists would kill himself at the first chance anyway and that incarceration would merely postpone the inevitable. But no one can say that anyone's suicide is truly inevitable. While the law cannot bring light to the depths at which a man contemplates his own destruction, it can render a service by making it as difficult as possible for him to do so. If incarceration for a short period can serve that purpose, and allow time for reflection, it will be worth while.

What should be done to a person who attempts to kill himself and kills someone else in the process—the doubtful marksman, for example, who aims the gun at his own head but kills his neighbor in the adjoining apartment? Unless we are to discard the sound principle that a man is held to intend the natural and probable consequences of his voluntary acts, the killer in such a case should be punished for murder or at least manslaughter. If a hunter accidentally kills another, he is not necessarily criminally responsible. Nor is every automobile driver who is involved in a fatal accident. But hunting and automobile driving are lawful, duly licensed activities. Attempting suicide, as yet, is not. It is a social and moral wrong. One who tries to kill himself should be held strictly accountable even for unforeseeable consequences resulting from the attempt. But one who jumps in the river in an unsuccessful effort to drown himself should not be criminally responsible for the death of one who dives in to rescue him but drowns in the process. The death of the rescuer was not directly caused by the suicide but rather was the product of the intervening voluntary act of the rescuer. However, the law should give the rescuer immunity for any injury he inflicts on the would-be suicide in the course of the rescue effort.[24]

Where a suicide is completed as part of a double-suicide pact and the partner to the pact survives, he should be punished for his own attempted suicide. If he aided and abetted the successful suicide of the other, he should be punished for murder or manslaughter, depending on his intent. The same result should follow when there was a murder-suicide pact. In that case one partner kills the other by agreement and then unsuccessfully attempts to take his own life. Clearly, he ought to be punished for the murder of his partner and for his own attempted suicide. If we exculpate the survivor of the murder-suicide pact, we say in effect that the deceased victim had the right to consent to his own murder. This is exactly the same principle involved in euthanasia, which is nothing more than assisted suicide. To admit the validity of the principle in a murder-suicide pact would be to concede its applicability in the wider area of voluntary euthanasia. The only reliable protection against the extension of the principle is to deny it completely. Similarly, the survivor of the double suicide pact, who actively aided and abetted the deceased partner in his suicide, as by providing him with the poison for that purpose, should be held criminally accountable. He did not murder his partner but he did aid and abet his suicide and it would be unsound to legitimize such conduct. It, too, would be a warrant for voluntary euthanasia.

The argument that one proposal cannot be accepted because it would lead to evil results is weak if it assumes that the initial step objected to is good or neutral in itself and is made bad only by the prospect of the extension of its principle into a bad result. The double-suicide or murder-suicide pact, however, is bad in itself. The argument that the exculpation of the survivor would lead to further bad extensions is merely cumulative. The pact is bad in itself for two reasons. On the pragmatic level, to recognize it would open a wide avenue for fraud and for murders designed to appear as suicide-by-pact. Secondly, it is wrong because, with few exceptions, a man does not have the legal right to consent to his own death. A man has a right to lay down his life to serve another. The suicide-by-consent, however, is not saving anyone's life. He is consenting to the termination of his life for some less important utilitarian reason, perhaps no more than that he is just tired of it all. Suicide by direct act is wrong and passive suicide by consent is also wrong in principle. Although there are few cases on the point, a majority of courts have ruled that a competent adult can be compelled to submit to a blood transfusion or other medical treatment that is necessary to save his life, even where the treatment is forbidden by the patient's religion.[25] Not even the First Amendment's paramount protection of the free exercise of religion can be used to cloak a passive suicide. But even if we were to conclude that a competent adult cannot be compelled to accept treatment, we do not thereby concede the lawfulness of suicide. To refuse necessary treatment is a form of suicide. So is a hunger strike. But the only form of suicide to which the law can attach a penalty for the attempt is suicide by affirmative act. The partner in a double-suicide or murder-suicide pact is not merely refusing to eat or to accept a blood transfusion. What he does is not merely an omission. Rather, he is subjecting himself at his own hand or that of his partner to a positive act of commission designed to kill him. Suicide, whether accomplished by action or inaction, flies in the face of the instinct for self-preservation, it deprives the community of a member on whom it was entitled to rely, and most importantly, it defies the will of the Creator who gives life and takes it away. Suicide is forbidden by nature no matter how we might wish "that the Everlasting had not fix'd his canon 'gainst self-slaughter!"[26]

Of course mere incarceration will frequently do no good unless it is coupled with treatment during the imprisonment and with careful attention for a time afterward. The following case summary illustrates the problem:

> In May, 1963, in Los Angeles, two men, Valdez and Wilde, each ingested approximately 50 sleeping capsules as part of a suicide pact. Wilde died but Valdez recovered. He was found guilty of aiding in the suicide of another under Section 401 of the California Penal Code and was sentenced to a term in the state prison. Upon his release from prison in September, 1963, Valdez returned to the scene of the previous suicide pact and ingested 100 sleeping capsules which killed him.[27]

According to many experts, the pattern of an approaching suicide is so recognizable and predictable that many suicides could be prevented by timely intervention. A number of agencies, such as the National Save-a-Life League, now provide assistance and consultation to troubled individuals at any hour of the day or night as well as long-range help in coping with the particular problems that drove them to consider suicide. These efforts are necessary and laudable. Suicides can be dissuaded, perhaps some for reasons no weightier than these from Dorothy Parker's *Résumé:*

> Razors pain you;
> Rivers are damp;
> Acids stain you;
> And drugs cause cramp;
> Guns aren't lawful;
> Nooses give;
> Gas smells awful;
> You might as well live.

Would that it were so easy. Generally the incipient suicide is a study in complexity. In 1967, the Center for Studies of Suicide Prevention was established in the National Institute of Mental Health. It publishes a periodical heralding the emergence of a new science, the *Bulletin of Suicidology.* A good beginning has been made. But a great deal needs to be done. And lives are at stake.

A sound policy, to promote respect for life, would aid these efforts to discourage suicide. It would offer help to those who contemplate or attempt their own destruction. It would penalize for their own good those who incorrigibly attempt the act. And it would promote a wider conviction that life is a stewardship, that Socrates was right when he said "a man should wait, and not take his own life until God summons him."[28] For even though there are ways that life can be forfeited, as in capital punishment, we have no right to work that forfeiture by suicide.

6

CAPITAL PUNISHMENT

"I'm scared," said Freddy Esherick, in his cell on Death Row in the Ohio State penitentiary. He was there because a jury convicted him of killing his father and trying to kill his mother. The jury of ten men and two women unanimously refused to recommend mercy. Freddy was born in 1951 to an unmarried couple who gave him to the local welfare board for adoption. He was placed with Fred Esherick, Sr., and his wife Aldona, who adopted him when he was fourteen months old. His parents were strict and "they were always on my back about smoking or something." Freddy had been involved in petty thievery but nothing really serious until the night of May 5, 1967, when Freddy was fifteen. On that night he killed his father with a bayonet, clubbed and nearly strangled his mother, and then stuffed her in the trunk of the family car with her husband's body. During the ride, Mrs. Esherick testified, "I called Freddy's name. I heard his voice say, 'You're in the trunk. Dad is dead and I'm going to kill you, too.'" Finally the boy stopped the car, dragged his mother and his father's body out of the trunk, and threw them down a nine-foot embankment into a river.[1] As of this writing, Freddy's execution has been stayed pending his appeal to the Supreme Court of the United States.

Why did the jury condemn this high school sophomore to die? One juror said:

> "I was for mercy at first, but the more we talked it over the more it seemed there just wasn't anything good about the boy. You just couldn't find anything about him that would deserve mercy.
> "He knew his mother was alive in that trunk and he dumped her in the river for dead. So I changed my mind and so did the others. I think there were about eight ballots."

Another juror reacted to the storm of indignation that followed the verdict:

> "It seems as if the jury is being found guilty. It seems the boy is getting a great deal of sympathy while the jury, which did its civic duty, is being portrayed as the guilty party."

When former Governor Theodore R. McKeldin of Maryland testified recently in favor of a bill to abolish the death penalty, he buried his face in his hands and said, "I am ashamed to say that I hanged four people, because I didn't have the character to do what I should have done. I yielded to the public clamor, and may God forgive me."[2]

How can anyone justify the calculated killing of another human being, even one who has himself taken a life? Supporters of the death penalty commonly claim that its existence deters potential murders and thereby saves lives. But this is easier to say than to prove.

In 1958 the state of Delaware abolished the death penalty for crime. It was reinstated in 1961. However, the first candidate for the gallows thereafter was a detective who killed his wife ten days after the death penalty was restored. The detective had long been an advocate of capital punishment. He was convicted of his crime and sentenced to a prison term. The existence of the death penalty did not deter this particular killer and it did not save his wife.[3]

Fourteen of the fifty states have now eliminated the death penalty or restricted it to special cases. The death penalty is authorized for a variety of federal crimes, ranging from murder to espionage and treason. The federal government has not executed anyone since 1963 and only four persons have been put to death by the federal government since 1955.[4] In 1966 only one person was executed in the United States and two were executed in 1967. In 1935 there were 199 executions and the number has been declining ever since.[5]

Opponents of capital punishment deny that it is an effective deterrent to crime. They can show that the removal of the death penalty for an offense has never been followed by a demonstrable increase of that particular crime. Indeed, the restoration of capital punishment is sometimes followed by an increase of crime. In more fundamental terms, those who would abolish the death penalty claim it violates the right to life, that life is given to man by the Creator and that man has no right to destroy the life of another. In the words of Governor McKeldin, "The vengeance that sends a man out of this world into eternity is not ours but the Lord's."[6]

Abolitionists also claim that no matter how exacting our criminal procedure, there remains the possibility of executing an innocent man. The late Archbishop Paul J. Hallinan of Atlanta, in calling executions "sordid substitutes for law, order, justice and human dignity," stated, "We know that the history of American penology is stained in the cases where the wrong man was fatally punished."[7] The finality of the penalty argues against taking that risk.

Some critics also maintain that the supreme penalty discourages convictions by juries who are reluctant to condemn a defendant to death. The result is that verdicts evade and distort the law to avoid condemning the defendant to death. One group of property owners in England, for example, petitioned in 1819 for the abolition of capital punishment for many of the minor offenses punished by death at that time. The group resolved, "Your Petitioners find by experience, that the infliction of death, or even the possibility of the infliction of death, prevents the prosecution, conviction and punishment of the criminal, and thus endangers the property which it is intended to protect."[8]

Opponents also argue that capital punishment tends to be reserved for the penniless and the friendless. The defendant with wealth or connections, it is said, can escape while the accused who cannot afford a high-priced lawyer more frequently faces the ultimate sanction.

We are concerned in this book with the diminishing respect for innocent life. The twentieth century has seen examples of this on a horrible scale. The natural reaction to perpetual war and to Nazi and Communist atrocities is to shrink from killing, to recoil from the death penalty as an avoidable expenditure of human life. Sydney Silverman, the sponsor of the 1964 bill to abolish capital punishment for murder in the United Kingdom, expressed this view in Parliament:

> "Sir Winston Churchill once described this twentieth century, which we began with so much hope, as 'this terrible twentieth century.' We have seen in it not merely those two wars, this destruction, this bloodshed. We have

seen whole cities of non-combatant men, women and children wiped out without notice at one blow. We have seen a nation collecting from the ends of the earth 6 million human beings not for any military purpose, but for annihilation on grounds of race or creed.

"We are living today in a world under the threat of human extinction. We may be beginning to make our way out of it. But who knows? It is impossible to argue that the execution or non-execution of two people in England every year can make a very great contribution to the improvement of a dark and menacing world. But in this darkness and gloom into which the twentieth century civilisation has so far led us, we can at least light this small candle and see how far its tiny beam can penetrate the gloom."[9]

The opponents of capital punishment thus argue that it does not deter, that it discourages convictions, that it bears most heavily upon the poor and friendless, that it entails a risk of irretrievable mistake, and finally, that it invades the divine prerogative. They are persuasive, as far as they go. However, they tend to concentrate only on part of the problem. It is frequently charged that those who would abolish capital punishment show more concern for criminals than they do for the actual and potential victims of crime. This type of argument is volatile and easily overstated. However, it does contain a basic truth that the abolitionists too often ignore. By the time the death penalty becomes an issue in a particular case, the victim is long deceased and the defendant is the center of attention. The hidden motivations that led to his horrible deed, the hardship and shame his execution would impose upon his innocent family, and kindred factors geared to evoke sympathy are emphasized in the press and on television. Perhaps we should guarantee equal time to the victim and to potential victims whose murders we ought to deter by all legitimate means. While the condemned prisoner is indeed in a terrible plight, it cannot be denied that, barring insanity, he brought it on himself. And we are entitled to presume that his late victim desired to live no less than he. But the victim is too often overlooked.

As author John Toland recently commented on the idealized film biography of hoodlums Bonnie Parker and Clyde Barrow:

But it was not [Texas Ranger Captain] Hamer who was made the hero of a film. Bonnie and Clyde were—a fact that I think tells us something about our age. On the day after the death of Bonnie and Clyde, the New York *Herald Tribune* observed editorially: "Society is glad that Louisiana rubbed them both out yesterday." Today we have become so "enlightened" that such phraseology strikes us as crude and unfeeling. Our attention and even our sympathy now seem focused not on the victim but on those who wield gun, knife and garrote—the murderers of *In Cold Blood*, the Boston Strangler, and Bonnie and Clyde. The victim has become faceless—the forgotten man.[10]

There is a real question as to whether capital punishment does in fact deter homicides. Of course, it finally deters further offenses by the criminal executed, but there are complications when we ask whether his execution deters others. Even if we assume or prove that the death penalty deters some potential murders, we must do more to justify it. Its deterrent effect must be sufficiently superior to other forms of punishment to warrant its retention despite the risk of mistake and its other shortcomings.

Those who would abolish capital punishment frequently show by statistics that the rate of homicides did not increase in a particular jurisdiction after abolition, or they show that the homicide rate in a jurisdiction that has the death penalty is just as high as the homicide rate in a jurisdiction that does not have it. However, statistics here are doubtful at best. For one thing, the formal abolition of capital punishment frequently follows a long period of disuse. In 1966 there was only one execution for crime in the entire United States, with two in 1967. No one has been executed in New Hampshire since 1939, in Montana since 1943, or in Massachusetts for more than twenty years.[11] Yet each of these states retains the death penalty. Comparisons of the crime rates among states are equally unsatisfactory. To evaluate data from different states we must take into account variances in the legal definitions of crimes, practices of the prosecuting authorities, court decisions, statistical procedures, and the wide range of political, social, economic, and moral conditions that could influence the crime rate. Exact comparisons, therefore, are impossible. It is similarly impossible to determine precisely the deterrent effect of any other punishment for any other crime. The Pennsylvania Legislative Committee on Capital Punishment concluded in 1961, "The plain fact is it can never be known how many persons are actually deterred by threat of punishment, whether capital or otherwise." Clearly, the difficulty of statistical proof should not lead us to abolish lesser punishments for lesser crimes. With the death penalty, too, we reach a point where the statistician must yield to the judgment of common sense and experience.

In the United Kingdom the Royal Commission on Capital Punishment (1949–53) found that the statistical argument for abolition is inconclusive:

> We have suggested that any deterrent effect of capital punishment is likely to reside primarily in its long-term effect on the attitude of society to murder rather than in the conscious calculations of potential criminals. If this is so, it cannot be expected that variations in the number of executions from year to year would be directly reflected in a rise or fall of the murder rate, and a failure to find any such correlations cannot properly be used as an argument against the view that the death penalty is a unique deterrent.
>
> The negative conclusion we draw from the figures does not of course imply a conclusion that the deterrent effect of the death penalty cannot be greater than that of any other punishment. It means only that the figures afford no reliable evidence one way or the other. It would no doubt be equally difficult to find statistical evidence of any direct relationship between the severity of any other punishment and the rise or fall of the crime to which it relates. Too many other factors come into the question.[12]

The basic weakness of the statistical argument here is that the figures show murders that were committed in spite of capital punishment, but they cannot show the murders that were deterred by it and therefore never committed. As J. Edgar Hoover once noted:

> The death penalty is a warning, just like a lighthouse throwing its beam out to sea. We hear about shipwrecks, but we do not hear about the ships the lighthouse guides safely on their way. We do not have proof of the number of ships it saves, but we do not tear the lighthouse down.[13]

In fact, it is even possible that the supreme penalty has the highest deterrent effect in those jurisdictions that continue to have high rates of homicide despite it. For the high homicide rate may be due to social and other factors that operate independently of the death penalty. That penalty may in fact operate to deter a substantial number of homicides that would otherwise be committed in that particular jurisdiction. The Joint Committee of the Canadian Parliament in 1956 found that the statistics indicate the death penalty actually does deter:

> The failures of capital punishment as a deterrent are obvious from the number of murders still committed. Its successes are unknown because it is impossible to determine the number of persons it has deterred from murder.

One measure of its deterrent effect was afforded by an analysis of murders which indicated that a considerable proportion, probably in excess of half, are committed under the compulsion of overwhelming passion or anger where no deterrent could have been effective. This would seem to demonstrate that the death penalty, coupled with the excellent standards of law enforcement prevailing in Canada, has been successful in deterring the commission of deliberate premeditated murders and reducing their incidence to minimum proportions. The deterrent effect may also be indicated by the widespread association of the crime of murder with the death penalty which is undoubtedly one reason why murder is regarded as such a grave and abhorrent crime.[14]

The death penalty is particularly effective in deterring criminals, particularly professionals, from carrying weapons and committing murders that might therefore put a fatal end to their own criminal careers. It is at least as likely that the criminal realizes only vaguely the remoteness of the chance that he actually would be executed. The Canadian Parliament Joint Committee Report in 1956 supported these conclusions,[15] and Monsignor George F. McKinney, Catholic chaplain at Sing Sing Prison, confirmed the point:

Of the hundreds of men I have interviewed, I found that 80 per cent of those implicated in a robbery failed to resort to violence because they feared the electric chair. . . . I would ask them "Why didn't you have the gun loaded—or why did you carry a toy pistol?" And they would usually say, "What, and stick my neck out for the electric chair?"[16]

Ultimately, the deterrent effect of capital punishment depends for its proof upon common sense and practical experience. The United Kingdom Royal Commission mentioned this case:

The Commissioner of Police of the Metropolis told us of a gang of armed shopbreakers who continued their operations after one of their members had been sentenced to death for murder and reprieved, but broke up and disappeared when, on a later occasion, two others were convicted of another murder and hanged. He thought it "a reasonable inference" that this was evidence of the uniquely deterrent effect of the death penalty; and that was the opinion of the police officers who dealt with the gang.[17]

Sir James Stephen, the nineteenth century's leading authority on criminal law, forcefully affirmed the inherent deterrence of the death penalty:

No other punishment deters men so effectually from committing crimes as the punishment of death. This is one of those propositions which it is difficult to prove, simply because they are in themselves more obvious than any proof can make them. It is possible to display ingenuity in arguing against it, but that is all. The whole experience of mankind is in the other direction. The threat of instant death is the one to which resort has always been made when there was an absolute necessity for producing some result. . . . No one goes to certain inevitable death except by compulsion. Put the matter the other way. Was there ever yet a criminal who, when sentenced to death and brought out to die, would refuse the offer of a commutation of his sentence for the severest secondary punishment? Surely not. Why is this? It can only be because "All that a man has will he give for his life." In any secondary punishment, however terrible, there is hope; but death is death; its terrors cannot be described more forcibly.[18]

Stephen wrote nearly one hundred years ago and his reference to the "threat of instant death" must be viewed in light of the long delays and uncertainties involved in the penal process today. Capital punishment is certainly not "instant." The procedure seems often interminable and this weakens the deterrent effect of the sanction. Sir James's psychological insights are still valid today. But society can profit from the death penalty, and innocent lives can be saved, only if its effect is not dissipated by intricacies and delays not required by justice.

The truth is that capital punishment does deter the commission of some homicides, although we cannot gauge the extent of the deterrent. Justice Samuel S. Leibowitz described a case in his court:

A thug went into a bar in South Brooklyn with a gun, held up three people there, and cowed them with his revolver.

He struck the proprietor with the butt end of the gun, inflicting minor wounds on his forehead, and fled.

The other day he pleaded guilty before me to robbery. I asked him these questions which I quote from the record:

THE COURT: I want to ask the defendant a question. Was the gun loaded?
THE DEFENDANT: No, your honor, I didn't want to hurt anybody.
THE COURT: You didn't want to kill anybody?
THE DEFENDANT: No, sir.
THE COURT: Why didn't you want to have a gun that was loaded?
THE DEFENDANT: Because I didn't want to hurt anybody.
THE COURT: Why?
THE DEFENDANT: Because I didn't want to go to the electric chair.[19]

It is interesting to note that in 1962 Judge Leibowitz defended capital punishment during a national television debate against Professor Thorsten Sellin of the University of Pennsylvania, one of the leading advocates of the statistical argument against the death penalty. In the debate, Professor Sellin made this revealing admission:

> "I haven't the slightest doubt that there may be some individuals who are deterred by the death penalty."[20]

The Canadian Association of Chiefs of Police argued from human nature as well as their own experience when they advocated the retention of the death penalty because:

> We sincerely believe that all sane persons would prefer a sentence of life imprisonment rather than suffer the death penalty, therefore, we feel that Capital Punishment is definitely an effective deterrent.[21]

While it cannot be argued that the death penalty should be retained merely as a morale-builder for police officers, their judgment is worthy of at least as much credence as that of the theorists who argue from statistics rather than from experience.

There can be no practical doubt that the death penalty does deter some criminals and does prevent the commission of some murders. Therefore, since it does save some innocent lives, the burden of proof ought to be on those who argue for its abolition. Unless a convincing case can be made for abolition, a proper regard for the sanctity of innocent life would dictate that the death penalty be preserved. It is fair to say that the abolitionists have not carried their burden and have not proven their case.

We must be careful, however, to distinguish the question of whether the death penalty can be basically justified from the procedural question of whether it is administered fairly. Too often these issues are confused. Rather, the proper response of a society concerned about protecting innocent life should be to affirm the right to inflict the death penalty and to implement it prudently while eliminating the procedural loopholes that permit the wealthy and highly placed to escape their punishment.

Let those who would argue in principle against the death penalty come forward and sustain their burden of proving that, despite its acknowledged efficacy in preserving some innocent human life, it ought to be discarded for a higher good. But let the supporters of capital punishment show that the niceties of criminal procedure are not so distorted as to result in unfair application. Monseignor Mc-Kinney of Sing Sing supported the elimination of capital punishment mainly because of the uneven way it was administered. He noted that if an accused cannot afford a top-flight lawyer his chances of receiving a death sentence are much higher:

> Or, if the person has some friends in high places or can get a group to back his cause, he has a chance to escape the electric chair. But the man with no money, no friends, or no group willing to take up his cause, stands a good chance of getting the chair.
>
> That is one of the reasons I felt the time was right for a change in the law. But we must wait to see if the change will work.[22]

If this unfairness of application were inherent in the death penalty, it ought to be abolished. But the unfairness is not inherent and the death penalty should not be abolished without seriously trying to eliminate the disparities that favor the wealthy or the organized criminal over the penniless and friendless defendant.

Capital punishment, however, should not be oversold by its supporteres as a deterrent. No punishment would be a deterrent for a crime of sudden passion or a crime committed by an insane person. The 1965 report of the Temporary Commission on Revision of the Penal Law and Criminal Code of the State of New York dealt with this question. The staff report prepared for that study noted that murder falls roughly into three categories: by reason of mental abnormality, as a result of emotionalism, or thirdly, for gain. The first two are largely undeterrable. It is principally in the third category that the deterrent effect of capital punishment can operate.

It is commonly agreed that punishment has three main purposes: reformation, deterrence and, to some extent, retribution. Obviously capital punishment excludes reformation of the executed criminal. There is, as we have seen, a difficult question as to whether the supreme penalty in fact deters. And in the controversy over deterrence we sometimes overlook the importance of retribution. Retribution here does not mean vengeance but rather reprobation. As Lord Justice Denning of the Royal Commission said:

> The punishment inflicted for grave crimes should adequately reflect the revulsion felt by the great majority of citizens for them. It is a mistake to consider the objects of punishment as being deterrent or reformative or preventive and nothing else. . . . The ultimate justification of any punish-

ment is not that it is a deterrent, but that it is the emphatic denunciation by the community of a crime: and from this point of view, there are some murders which, in the present state of public opinion, demand the most emphatic denunciation of all, namely the death penalty.[23]

This function of the death penalty in generating community abhorrence for murder was described in detail by the Royal Commission:

We have been told that the first thing a murderer says when he is arrested is often "Shall I be hanged?" or "I did it and I am ready to swing for it," or something of that kind. What is the inference to be drawn from this? Clearly not that the death penalty is an effective deterrent, for he has not been deterred; nor that he consciously considered the risk of the death penalty and accepted it; still less that the death penalty was not so effective a deterrent as some other punishment might have been. The true inference seems to us to be in the popular imagination. We think it is reasonable to suppose that the deterrent force of capital punishment operates not only by affecting the conscious thoughts of individuals tempted to commit murder, but also by building up in the community, over a long period of time, a deep feeling of peculiar abhorrence for the crime of murder. "The fact that men are hung for murder is one great reason why murder is considered so dreadful a crime." This widely diffused effect on the moral consciousness of society is impossible to assess, but it must be at least as important as any direct part which the death penalty may play as a deterrent in the calculations of potential murderers. It is likely to be specially potent in this country where the punishment for lesser offences is much more lenient than in many other countries, and the death penalty stands out in the sharper contrast.[24]

The fact is that there are some crimes so atrocious that they deserve no penalty less severe than death. On January 15, 1961, Rose Marie Riddle, a small, blonde six-year-old, was kidnaped, brutally raped, and murdered in Shafter, California. The deed was done by one Richard Arlen Lindsey and his wife Dixie. Mrs. Lindsey, herself pregnant, watched her husband lure the innocent child into his car. Mrs. Lindsey then sat in the car and watched her husband brutally attack the girl, who screamed hopelessly for her life. Indeed, after her husband had completed his brutal assault, it was the wife who killed the child by smashing her skull with a tire iron. Mr. Lindsey was convicted of first-degree murder and kidnaping and he was executed at San Quentin Prison on November 14, 1961. His wife pleaded guilty to charges of kidnaping and murder and received a sentence of life imprisonment. We may rightly ask what penalty would have sufficed for a crime of this magnitude. Or consider the assassination of a president or a senator. We may conclude, too, that the deterrence of such crimes is a goal so important that we ought to employ any legitimate means reasonably calculated to achieve that deterrent.

The main justification for the death penalty is precisely this: that it uniquely promotes respect for innocent life. As Canadian Minister of Justice E. Davie Fulton put it:

> Society's concern for its basic rules is expressed in its commands and corresponding sanctions that together constitute our criminal law. The degree of society's concern with respect to individual rules is reflected in the method of expression adopted.
>
> In this sense, therefore, the sanction for the law against murder may properly reflect the importance which society attaches to the maintenance of that law. In our view, Canadians properly attach so high a value to the sanctity of human life that the law which translates this feeling into effective form should provide the maximum sanction for its deliberate breach, and no other penalty would be considered adequate.[25]

It is only when we attach the ultimate penalty to its commission that we stigmatize murder as the crime of crimes. Over the long run, we aim to implant a public conviction that this crime is different from all others precisely because it is the taking of innocent human life. This climate of abhorrence could not be achieved through lesser penalties. Life imprisonment without parole has been suggested as an alternative to capital punishment, but this has several drawbacks. The cost of maintaining convicted murderers in prison for life without parole, incidentally, is not one of the drawbacks and is of no consequence in this matter involving life itself. Indeed, such prisoners could be made self-supporting to a considerable extent. But life imprisonment without hope of release can be more cruel than the death penalty. As one crime reporter asked:

> Of what use is it to commute the death sentence of a man, to relieve him of the horror of waiting in a small "holding" cell hard by the room of execution, and to present him with the gift of life—if he is to spend that gift in a grey, hopeless world behind prison walls?[26]

Also, the abolitionists are not content with life terms without parole. They tend to favor routine parole for convicted murderers. As soon as it appeared likely that an abolition bill would pass in

England, a movement was commenced in favor of shorter terms of imprisonment for murders. So the abolitionists are not merely agitating against the death penalty. They are contending for a further reduction of penalties. In practice, total life imprisonment rarely exists any more and life terms will tend to become shorter. In California, for instance, the average time served on a life sentence is twelve years.[27] A committee of the American Bar Association has proposed that maximum sentences for felonies should not exceed five years in most cases and "As an outside limit for extreme cases, twenty-five years ought to be the maximum authorized prison term."[28] The public's memory is short and a few years after the crime the tendency would be to favor parole for the convicted murderer rather than a continuation of a hopeless life sentence. The net effect could only be a lessening of the respect for human life.

In recent years crime has risen rapidly but prison populations have been declining. In 1961 Americans committed 1.93 million serious crimes. In 1965 the figure had risen to 2.78 million. Yet the prison population actually declined from 220,149 in 1961 to 211,150 in 1965. The difference is attributable in part to greater leniency in parole and probation policies and the trend continues.[29] There is much to be said for flexible and humane parole and probation policies. But the point to remember here is that, because of the trend toward more crime and less punishment, the abolition of the death penalty will tend to introduce routine parole for murderers. If murderers are granted parole as readily as those who commit larceny or bigamy or simple assault, the public abhorrence of the crime of murder will have become a thing of the past. Instead, there will develop an unspoken conviction that murder, the taking of innocent life, is no different in kind from the taking of money or any other crime.

It is argued, too, that the death penalty should be discarded because the condemned killer often suffers more excruciating terrors of anticipation than the agonies suffered by his victim. Also, as the 1962 United Nations report, "Capital Punishment," noted:

> Moreover, the penalty of death is a form of cruelty and inhumanity unworthy of a civilization which claims to be humane; doctors report that even the most efficient methods do not result in instantaneous and painless death.[30]

But, it is fair to ask, why is it wrong if the deliberate, premeditated murderer suffers more than his victim? So long as the method of execution is as painless and as instantaneous as science can devise, we ought to be concerned less with this factor than with the task of preventing future murders of innocent persons.

The claim is made that if we are going to have a deterrent objective in administering the death penalty, then we should hold executions in Yankee Stadium or at the Washington Monument, with the maximum publicity and with the maximum attendance of spectators. This argument, however, misses the point. For the deterrent effect of the death penalty does not reside in its effect upon those who actually witness the execution or relay their firsthand accounts to their friends and acquaintances. Rather the deterrent effect is found in the cultivation of a sense of dread in the community at the implementation of this most awful sanction.

The strongest argument against the death penalty is the chance of an irrevocable mistake. It should require an extraordinary certainty of guilt to justify such an irreversible sanction. While the possibility of error does not undermine the theoretical case in support of the right of the state to impose capital punishment, it does raise serious roadblocks in the way of its use. Unless we have eliminated the possibility of error as far as we can, prudence and a proper regard for the human life we are trying to exalt would counsel against the use of the supreme penalty in the case in question.

Today, the danger is not so much that we are liable to execute an innocent man but rather that some guilty persons will suffer the supreme penalty while others, no less guilty than they, will escape punishment because the Supreme Court has ensnarled the criminal process in a network of artificial restrictions that place a premium on blind chance and the resourcefulness of lawyers.

Since 1958 serious crime has increased at a rate almost nine times the growth of the nation's population. Major crimes increased 88% from 1960 to 1967. In this period murders increased by 51%, a figure that reflects not only a breakdown of law and order but also a growing disregard for innocent human life.

As Notre Dame law professor G. Robert Blakey said, in a speech to the National District Attorneys Association:

"People are looking more and more to law enforcement as a catch-all, as the school, the home and the church break down its sources of discipline. But law enforcement isn't there any more. It collapsed some time ago, but the realization hasn't caught up with us yet. We are still working under a system that was devised hundreds of years ago in England. It has not worked in our complex society."[31]

Judicial interpretations are responsible to a great extent for the soaring crime rate. The Supreme Court of the United States has decreed impractical rules governing apprehension, search and seizure, interrogation, habeas corpus, and other aspects of criminal procedure. These court-ordained rules are grotesque in their adherence to rigid formalisms and in their disregard for the basic question of guilt or innocence. The right of law-abiding citizens to live in reasonable safety and peace is insufficiently considered. This judicial trend has drawn well-deserved criticism from leaders of the bar and law enforcement officials. It was not without reason that former commissioner of the New York City Police, Michael J. Murphy, protested that, owing to court interpretations, "we are forced to fight by Marquis of Queensberry rules, while the criminals are permitted to gouge and bite." New York County District Attorney Frank S. Hogan recently complained that the Supreme Court's rulings had "significantly increased the chances that a criminal will escape judgment."

The basic vice of the Supreme Court's rigid decisions is that they have obscured the question of guilt or innocence. In the famous Miranda case in 1966,[32] the Supreme Court imposed restrictions on police interrogation of suspects more severe than in any other Western or even civilized nation in the world.[33] After the Supreme Court reversed his conviction, Ernesto A. Miranda was retried and was convicted after a nine-day trial. He would have gone free, however, had not the county attorney's office learned of an alleged statement by Miranda to a friend that he had committed the rape of which he was accused. Most of the nine-day trial was taken up with legalistic discussions of the Supreme Court's rulings and virtually no attention was paid to the question of whether Miranda was guilty or innocent. The presiding judge, Laurence T. Wren, said, "When the verdict was finally in, I suddenly realized, with complete amazement and infinite disgust, that we had not dealt at all during the nine-day trial with the basic question of guilt or innocence." As a matter of fact, in open court, but with the jury excluded, Miranda had taken the witness chair and admitted to the judge that he had raped the girl. Judge Wren expressed consternation at the thought that the jury, having been deprived of Miranda's formal confession, might well have acquitted him. He wondered how the jury would have felt if it had acquitted Miranda because of the technicalities of the Supreme Court's rulings, and then had learned that, out of the hearing of the jury, Miranda had confessed his guilt in open court, in a confession which because of the absurd legalistic rules was not available for consideration by the jury.[34]

The effect of the Supreme Court's erratic rulings is most clearly evident in Washington, D.C., where the 1957 case of Mallory v. United States curtailed the right of District of Columbia police to interrogate suspects.[35] Mallory's confession was held inadmissible solely because it occurred eight hours after his apprehension. He was not coerced or physically abused. But the Court ruled that the failure of the police to seek a magistrate to arraign him until after his confession constituted the "unnecessary delay" in arraignment forbidden by the Federal Rules of Criminal Procedure. Mallory v. U.S. was followed by a virtual crime explosion. In 1957 there were 15,554 crimes reported in the District of Columbia, a reduction from the 1950 total of 20,163. The clearance rate in 1957 was 49.5% of the crimes compared with 48.5% in 1950. The situation, therefore, had achieved a certain stability and was in a major sense improving. However, by 1966, after the Supreme Court had been working on the problem for nine years, the number of offenses had more than doubled to 34,765, while the clearance rate had dropped to a scandalous 26.3%. This record impelled the Congress to enact a statute in 1967 to restore a limited but more realistic right of interrogation to the District of Columbia police.[36] The Federal Crime Control Act of 1968[37] affirmed this right to interrogate suspects for a reasonable period and it extended it to federal courts generally. The 1968 Act also provided that, in federal trials, confessions shall be admitted in evidence if voluntary and shall not be automatically excluded merely because the suspect was not fully advised of his rights. These enactments will be helpful, provided they survive the scrutiny of the

Supreme Court. However, they do not apply to prosecutions in state courts.

The statistics compiled by the Federal Bureau of Investigation show that most serious crimes are committed by repeaters, who are often enabled to continue their careers in crime by judicial leniency. Since 1963, 75% of all persons charged with crime before federal law enforcement authorities have had a record of two or more arrests. Of the 965 persons who were acquitted or whose cases were dismissed in federal courts in 1963, the FBI found that 83% had been rearrested on new charges by June of 1966. In state prosecutions, 67% of those who commit burglary are rearrested for subsequent crimes; 66% of those who commit auto theft; 65% of those who commit serious assault; 60% of those who are arrested for narcotics violations; 56% of those arrested for forgery and 42% of those charged with robbery.

Lenient and unrealistic parole and probation policies are also responsible for a large share of the crime increase. Of all the criminals freed in 1963 on parole from federal prisons, 82% were rearrested for new crimes by June of 1966; 47% of those who, in federal courts, were given probation or suspended sentences in 1963 were rearrested within thirty months. As one law enforcement official in a large United States city complained recently, "If I could lock up just 700 people tonight, it would eliminate 90% of the crime in this city tomorrow." Instead of addressing themselves to these real problems of law enforcement and the breakdown of our judicial machinery, many who indiscriminately bewail the plight of the criminal defendant complain that crime is caused by poverty, that society and not the criminal is at fault. This conclusion is wholly unsupported by the observable data.[38] Unfortunately they carry this fallacious theory and their disregard for sound law enforcement into the controversy over capital punishment. For this reason the issue of whether to retain the death penalty cannot be considered only on its immediate merits. Rather, it must be viewed in regard to these over-all problems of the general denial of personal accountability.

Clearly, something must be done if we are to avoid the disintegration of our criminal process. Perhaps an answer will be found in amending the Fifth Amendment to the United States Constitution, which protects persons against being compelled to testify against themselves. Some lawyers, including the noted defense lawyer Percy Foreman, have recommended that defendants be required to answer questions put to them by the judge in open court in the presence of the jury. If the defendant refused to answer a question, the jury could draw its own conclusion. Unfortunately, the Supreme Court has contrived to give poor defendants the same loopholes as the rich, rather than attempting to close the loopholes for all persons. The tightening of procedures, with the elimination of the unnecessarily rigid technicalities decreed by the Supreme Court, is a task of the highest urgency. But as long as criminal procedure is so favorable to the defendant, we can ill afford to weaken law enforcement. We should, therefore, put aside the thought of eliminating capital punishment. In the meantime, however, the courts should scrutinize capital cases carefully to minimize any unfair advantages enjoyed by the wealthy and the highly placed and to afford the poor and friendless defendant a fair and comparable hearing.

Apart from a general rebirth of realism on the Supreme Court, some things can be done to make the death penalty more workable. It might be worth while, for example, to provide that no person can be sentenced to death unless the jury and the judge both concur, not only in his guilt but also in the application of the death penalty. There ought to be a two-stage procedure in the trial of capital cases such as New York and some other states have.[39] The jury should consider first the question of guilt or innocence and then separately the question of penalty. The two issues are logically separate, and for the jury to decide the penalty at the same time as it decides that the defendant did in fact commit the crime can result in prejudice to the defendant. It would be wise to endow appellate courts with the power to review not only the question of guilt or innocence but also the wisdom of the death sentence.[40] Ultimately the governor of the state also has authority to commute death sentences. While the power of commutation should be sparingly used, it can be an effective added safeguard against arbitrary decisions.

Generally the death penalty ought to be reserved for deliberate and willful murder done with premeditation or in the course of committing a felony, treason as narrowly defined in the Constitution, requiring an overt act proven by two witnesses, and wartime sabotage or espionage. All are offenses that substantially and deliberately impair innocent life.

The net effect of these restrictions would be to limit the application of the death penalty to exceptional cases. But the right and power of the state to impose the ultimate sanction would be recognized and preserved. This is crucially important in the matter of homicide. Prudently applied, capital punishment would deter homicide and save lives. And it would enhance the sanctity of innocent life through the cultivation of a community abhorrence of murder as the detestable crime of crimes.

In treating abortion, euthanasia, suicide, and capital punishment, we confront a modern tendency to cheapen innocent life by a disregard for sound principles that ought to govern the termination of life in those matters. But the basic irresponsibility that is evident in those areas has a common source. It affects the prevailing attitudes toward the origin of life as well as its termination. Nowhere is this more evident than in the current obsession with contraception. The practice of sterilization raises similar questions. As we seek to plumb the meaning of the reigning irresponsibility, it is appropriate at this point to consider the nature and implications of the phenomenon of birth control.

7

CONTRACEPTION

The Pretext

HAVE YOU EVER BEEN MUGGED?
WELL, YOU MAY BE.

So began a typical full-page advertisement in the New York *Times* sponsored by a group called the Campaign to Check the Population Explosion. Above the caption was a picture of a middle-aged, be-spectacled man gasping in a headlock clamped on him by a mugger. The mugger held a knife at the victim's throat. Lest you get the wrong idea, the text of the advertisement informs us that the remedy for this sort of thing is—not police, but birth control:

> There is an aggravated assault in this country every 3 minutes. A forcible rape every 26 minutes. A murder every hour—11,000 a year. . . .
>
> This has come with the population explosion in the United States, where our numbers have doubled—from 100 million people to more than 200 million people—in the lifetime of many of us.
>
> City slums—jam-packed with juveniles, thousands of them idle—breed dis-content, drug addiction and chaos. And crime in the cities is not the only problem. We have air and water pollution in wide areas. And the quality of life in this great country of ours is deteriorating before our eyes with the rapid increase of people.
>
> *Is there an answer? Yes—birth control is one.*
>
> And the quicker the better. For the population explosion if not checked will compound itself—adding millions of idle youngsters to our streets—in just a few short years.[1]

The idea seems to be that most criminals are people and if we reduce the numbers of people, why, the crime problem will disap-pear. The taxpayer, too, would benefit:

> A fraction of the vast amounts we spend on health and welfare if devoted to birth control could help check our skyrocketing numbers. And incidentally,

help balance the badly imbalanced national budget and save money for hard-pressed taxpayers.

Readers of the ad are urged to write to government officials to urge *"a crash program* for population stabilization." And the ad closes with a pointed appeal to residents of the inner city:

Do it *now*. Before you walk home tonight.

This advertisement is worth noting here not because it makes any sober contribution to our understanding of the population problem: on the contrary, its unreasoning appeal to fear and its flaming rhetoric can only confuse and mislead. But it is useful to mention it here because it shows the ingenuity of those who advance even crime in the streets as a serious justification for birth control.

There are three basic methods of birth prevention, apart from total or partial abstinence from sexual intercourse. They are abortion, sterilization, and contraception. The term "contraception" is generally understood not to include periodic abstinence from intercourse, the only method of family planning sanctioned by the Catholic Church. In recent years birth control has been urged primarily as a way to check an alarming increase in the world's population. In 1798 the Rev. Thomas Robert Malthus, in his "Essay on the Principle of Population," stated that population tends to increase geometrically while the means of subsistence increase only arithmetically. The outcome, he concluded, is inevitable poverty and disaster. In Malthus' time the world population was approximately 900 million. In 1830 it was 1 billion. By 1950 it had risen to 2.5 billion. In 1960 it was 3 billion and it now is estimated at 3.5 billion. At the current growth rates, world population will double again by the year 2000. From the beginning of the world until 1930, the population of the world reached a level of only 2 billion. But in the following century, from 1930 to 2030, it is estimated that it will multiply seven times to 14 billion if present trends continue. Every day 324,000 new babies are born in the world. Ten thousand die each day from starvation or malnutrition and 123,000 from other causes—a net daily gain of about 190,000 people. The largest increase in population is in the "have not" nations, owing partly to the reduction of death rates brought about by medical advancements.[2]

The following figures show the density of population in 1965 and the density expected by 2000:[3]

	POPULATION PER SQUARE MILE	
	1965	2000
Asia	108	202
Africa	26	65
Europe	167	192
Latin America	31	78
North America	26	41
Oceania (Australia, New Zealand, etc.)	5	10

The population increase in some parts of the world is alarming. It is compounded by the fact that food supplies have not everywhere kept pace. Within the next twenty years some underdeveloped areas will be faced with actual famine if present population trends and production inadequacies continue. However, the problem is not simply one of overpopulation. In some parts of the world economic stagnation is caused by underpopulation. In some countries the task is one of encouraging people to relocate away from too heavily concentrated areas. And the essential task throughout the world is to increase food production. The real issues, unfortunately, have been obscured by those who ignore them in their single-minded urging of birth control as the premier solution.

We cannot wish away the critical problems of overcrowding in some parts of the earth. But we can do something about feeding people and developing barren areas to accommodate them. The science of agriculture has made it possible for us to conquer hunger regardless of population growth. As economist Barbara Ward put it:

> Even if the rate of population growth goes on at its present vertiginous rate, we can still feed the human race in the foreseeable future. Remember, this is the first time in the whole of man's history in which it has been possible to say this.[4]

A similar point was made by Dr. Harrison Brown of California Institute of Technology:

> Given the necessary technology, which I am convinced can be developed, the earth has ample resources to enable persons the world over to lead abundant lives.[5]

The agricultural resources of the world have not been used to their maximum potential. Cows in America yield ten times as much milk as do the cows in Asia. The world average yield for wheat is 15 bushels per acre. In Denmark, however, the Danes get 40 bushels per acre from their soggy, sandy soil.[6] The Atomic Energy Commission is studying the construction of giant agro-industrial complexes built around nuclear reactors as a means of providing food and jobs to millions of people in underdeveloped countries.[7] Fertilizers, too, are an essential weapon in the fight against hunger. Secretary of Agriculture Orville Freeman recently emphasized that "world fertilizer consumption must increase from today's estimated 7 million tons a year to 47 million tons, a prospective market expansion from a billion dollars today to 7 billion dollars a year by 1980."[8]

We have hardly begun to tap the resources of the sea. Scientists have perfected a clinically pure fish concentrate with a protein content of 80%. This fish flour is inexpensive and easy to make.[9] Secretary of the Interior Stewart Udall described it as a "lifeline to the future of the world's hungry millions."[10] While we cannot say that the fish flour is the single solution to the food problem, it does illustrate the potential resources still locked in the sea. Only 1% of the world's food now comes from the sea and 98% of that quantity comes from the small seas of the Northern Hemisphere.[11] These are merely a few examples of our ability to produce more food.

Apart from the issue of food production, the extent of the population increase itself has too often been obscured by superficial analysis. India is often cited as the prime example of an overpopulated country. About 21 million babies are born in India every year. Deaths are 8 million, giving India a net growth of 13 million every year, more than the entire population of Australia.[12] The Indian population is now well in excess of half a billion and it is expected to pass the billion mark by 1994. The population of Communist China, incidentally, is expected to reach the billion mark by 1985.[13] It is an oversimplification, however, to regard India as teeming with people incredibly packed together. India has a population density of 374 people per square mile. Yet England has 577 per square mile and the Netherlands 767. These countries maintain a standard of living higher than India's. While their higher standards cannot be said simply to be caused by high population density, that density has not prevented the improvement of the living conditions in those countries. It is likely that the main reason why England and the Netherlands are better off than India lies in their economic organization and trade, as well as in their geographic situation. They do prove, however, that mere density of population does not preclude prosperity.

Unfortunately it is difficult to visualize how many people there actually are in the world. Most people would be surprised to know that if you took all the people in the world and gave each one six square feet of ground to stand on, they would all fit into about four fifths of Suffolk County, which covers the eastern half of Long Island, New York, and there would be 168 square miles left over. Or they would all fit into about three fifths of the area of Rhode Island. Clearly the problem is not simply one of a world-wide density of population. Rather, it involves the efficiency with which we use our land and other resources. Also, natural tendencies toward population limitation must be considered. One could make simplistic projections of current birth rates and envision a world filled with people, standing elbow to elbow and nudging each other into the sea. But nature does not work that way. The mother herring lays so many eggs that if each one grew up to be a mother herring and to lay eggs all the seas would be solid herring eggs in three years. There are natural factors that inhibit the unchecked growth of the herring population and there are factors that operate to restrain what is called the human population explosion. Some of the current prophets of doom unfortunately are reminiscent of the old Roman, Tertullian, who lamented, around A.D. 200:

> The highest testimony is matter of common knowledge: We are burdensome to the world. The elements scarcely suffice us. Our needs press. There are complaints among all. For now nature will not support us. Pestilence, famine, wars, and the swallowing up of cities are depicted, indeed, as remedies, as haircuts for the growth of the human race.[14]

Similarly, St. Jerome concluded nearly two centuries later that "The world is already full and the earth does not hold us."[15]

The tendency of the modern birth controllers is to mistake inadequate production for an excess of population:

> When the nomadic Indians roamed the uncultivated plains of North America

before the coming of these immigrants, the entire country with its estimated Indian population of only 500,000 and its shortage of food, would have been regarded as "overpopulated" according to the norms of the exponents of Planned Parenthood. Yet, the same plains today are being retired into a "land bank" because they are overproductive in a land of 175 million.[16]

The fact is that in many parts of the world birth rates are declining sharply. The birth rate in the United States is lower than it was in the depression years of the 1930s. In 1957 the birth rate reached a peak of 122.9 live births for each 1000 women aged fifteen through forty-four. In 1966 it dropped to 92.9. In 1967 it fell to 88.8, the lowest level in twenty-two years.[17] Interestingly, there has been a steady decline in births and a persistent rise in the marriage rate in this country since 1961, indicating an increasing practice of birth control by married couples.[18] There are indications, however, that the number and proportion of women in the reproductive years will rise sharply over the next fifteen years.[19] This could reverse the declining birth rate in the United States, unless the normal fertility is curtailed by the use of contraceptives. Incidentally, the falling birth rate in the United States cannot be blamed simply on the pill. The decline began after the peak year of 1957 and contraceptive pills did not come into wide use until four years later. There is no doubt, though, that the pill has added some impetus to the decline. Dr. Donald J. Bogue, past president of the Population Association of America, says the primary reason for the sharp recent decline in the American birth rate is that "the American population knows how to control fertility. Surveys show that knowledge of birth control is almost 100 per cent. This puts our national birth rate completely under control, so to speak. People can manipulate it up or down according to the prevailing mood. The present mood seems to be toward smaller families."[20] Significantly, according to Dr. Bogue, the white birth rate in the United States is nearly down to the level of replacement. He foresees that the greater use of contraceptives by Negroes will cause a similar decline in the Negro birth rate in the next few years.

In the effort to curb the population increase, birth control has become a central element of public policy in many countries. In Turkey, roving government teams induce women to receive a plastic intrauterine device. The goal of the Turkish government is to reduce the annual population increase from 3% to 2%, which would bring it into line with the rate of increase in the United States.[21] In Pakistan, 150 trained Lady Family Planning Visitors travel the countryside, inserting intrauterine devices into any woman who will accept them. In East Pakistan, 65 million people are crowded into an area the size of Illinois and 80 million are expected by 1975. The goal of President Muhammad Ayub Khan's program is to reduce the annual population increase from 3% to 2.5% by 1970.[22] India's health minister has proposed, so far unsuccessfully, that parents with three or more children be compulsorily sterilized. In the meantime, the Indian government is making all the known effective methods of population control available to the people and is making great efforts to induce them to use one means or another. Family-planning workers in India are increasingly relying on voluntary sterilization as the preferable contraceptive means.

An imaginative contraceptive technique was proposed by the governor of central Java, who suggested mass entertainments for villages so that people would not go to bed too early.[23] This is on a par with Al Capp's suggestion that the answer to world hunger can be found in the Shmoos, of Li'l Abner fame:

> A shmoo lays both milk *and* eggs—all neatly packaged and labelled "Grade A". Broiled, a shmoo tastes like *steak*—fried it comes out *chicken*—and all *white meat!* There's no waste. Shmoo whiskers make sturdy toothpicks, and its eyeballs make splendid suspender buttons.
>
> It is not cruel to eat a shmoo. Shmoos *love* to be eaten. At the slightest sign of interest a shmoo will fling itself into the nearest skillet and *broil itself to a turn!!*[24]

A proposal of similar magnitude was seriously advanced by Dr. William Shockley, Nobel prize-winning physicist, and a professor at Stanford University. His novel idea would enlist the resources of the Stock Exchange:

> All young girls under his system would be temporarily sterilized by a time capsule contraceptive—a silicon sponge providing slow seepage of a contraceptive hormone placed under the skin. When married, the girl and her husband would be issued 22 certificates, 10 of which would be needed for capsule removal to permit a birth.
>
> The couple then could, after two births, either sell their remaining two certificates or buy more on the Stock Exchange and have a third child.[25]

In Communist Cuba any woman who requests it can obtain free contraceptive assistance from the public health services. Fidel Castro, however, has attacked the United States Government for promoting family planning in underdeveloped countries. The American concern over rising population, he says, demonstrates "imperialism's lack of faith in the future."[26] Nevertheless, the Cuban medical profession has come to regard family planning as a public-health necessity because of the growing prevalance of abortion. However, while the Cuban government will provide women with intrauterine devices or with diaphragms made in eastern Europe, it will not provide contraceptive pills because the Cuban doctors are not convinced that they are safe. In Mexico the high incidence of abortion has led some clinics run by the Mexican government, which otherwise is not involved in family planning, to offer contraceptive assistance as an alternative to abortion.[27]

In Japan the birth rate has been cut in half, so that it has been 1% or less per year for the past decade.[28] This reduction has been achieved under the impetus of a "eugenic protection" law passed in 1948. The law officially sanctioned birth control by contraceptive devices and made abortion legal on limited grounds, such as rape, probable defect of the child, and health hazards to the mother. Amendments to the law in 1949 and 1952 authorized abortion on economic grounds and made it much easier to obtain. It is estimated that one out of every three pregnancies in Japan is now terminated by abortion. Officially reported abortions total nearly a million a year and it is estimated that a comparable number are unreported. About 10% of the nation's doctors are authorized to perform abortions and they have strongly opposed full government approval of the contraceptive pill, which would reduce the pregnancies, abortions, and the doctors' income.[29] Increasingly, concern is voiced in Japan that the nation's population-control program is so successful that the population is not even replenishing itself. In 1965 the Health and Welfare Ministry reported in a white paper that the net reproduction rate had fallen below 1.0. The net reproduction rate is a measure to gauge long-term trends of population development. It is a comparison between the number of women in the childbearing years and the female infants born during a single year who will eventually replace the women of childbearing age, taking into account the anticipated losses from mortality. When the rate dips below 1.0 this indicates the population is no longer reproducing itself. In Japan's case the rate has been around or below 1.0 since 1956.[30] Nor is this phenomenon limited to Japan. A similar situation exists in European countries such as Sweden, Norway, France, and England.[31] The birth rate in the Soviet Union has fallen by 60% in the last forty years.[32]

It is important not to belittle the population crisis. However, there is reason to believe that population growth, far from being an evil, is actually a good of which some underdeveloped countries are very much in need. Oxford University economist Colin Clark claims that "Population growth is the driving force behind economic growth. Stopping the so-called population explosion in countries like India will also halt economic growth."[33] "The problem in underdeveloped countries is not overpopulation but underpopulation," says Dr. Luis Bramao, head of the World Soil Office of the United Nations Food and Agriculture Organization.[34] Dr. Bramao, a leading soil expert, developed this idea as follows: "You are surprised to hear me say that what underdeveloped countries suffer from is underpopulation. The reason is that only where there is what is supposed to be overpopulation are there enough people to make a good beginning towards a higher standard of life. Take Brazil, for example, how can you develop a country like Brazil when it has a population of only 80 million?"

The 80 million population of Brazil would be equivalent to a population in France of only 500,000. "And where would France be today if she had so few?" asked Dr. Bramao. He continued:

> There is only one inhabitant per square kilometer in Mato Grosso, Brazil's largest state, where the soil potential is tremendous. But who is going to cultivate it?
>
> Naturally, the standard of living is low. If you want a high standard of living, you must go to the highly populated countries. The Netherlands is an extreme example, with 358 persons per square kilometer, yet it has a high living standard.
>
> Or take your own United States. In the past 30 years its population has increased around 60 million. Food production is 60 per cent higher than in 1930 with 80 per cent less crop area and using less than one-half as many farm man-hours. . . .
>
> Many things stand in the way of development. It isn't just a question of

soil and water. To solve the problem on a world basis will require education, capital and marketing development. In addition there are socio-economic and religious factors which must be taken into account. Undoubtedly, Pope Paul had these things in mind when he called on the UN to multiply bread for the tables of mankind.

The emphasis on increased production is not at all limited to those who oppose contraception. Dr. Shiroshi Nasu of Tokyo University favors birth control to limit population growth. But he emphasizes that greater production is the immediate answer to the population explosion he fears:

> The control of population growth, although it might become a kind of necessity in the future, cannot be depended upon too much now as the major means of adjusting the unbalanced food and population relationship.
> As the adoption of birth control among the developing nations will presuppose a raised standard of living, a wider diffusion of education as well as a changed mental outlook, it will certainly take many years to come. During this time, the predicted crisis will not stop approaching.
> It will be a race between the two, and our prospect of winning the race is not too bright at present.
> So we have to turn our attention toward the increase of food production.[35]

In summary, the theory that the population explosion is a simplistic excuse for massive birth control cannot withstand analysis. The specter of an overcrowded world has been used to make contraception respectable and even a civic duty. Moreover, this has occurred in areas, such as our own country, where the rhetoric about teeming, starving millions is largely irrelevant. If we would understand the growth of contraception in its proper context, that is, as an incident of a more basic flight from responsibility, we must first realize that there is no crisis of numbers sufficiently pervasive or compelling to justify the increasing prevention of new life. Rather the increase of birth control, and particularly of contraception, is an independent phenomenon with roots more basic than a numbers game.

The Practice

In December 1967 thirty heads of government presented to Secretary General U Thant a Declaration on Population by World

Leaders, in which they warned of the perils of overpopulation and called for family planning to be a recognized and basic human right. The signers, including President Lyndon B. Johnson, emphasized that the "great majority of parents desire to have the knowledge and the means to plan their families."[36] The Declaration was not an official act of the United Nations, but it was warmly received by Mr. Thant and the whole affair was generally interpreted as placing the moral authority of the United Nations behind the Declaration. Although the United Nations generally does not give financial aid for family planning efforts, a number of its agencies disseminate advice for that purpose and the United Nations Economic and Social Council has approved the granting of financial aid for birth control projects. Oddly, it has frequently been the resistance of the Soviet Union as well as of such Catholic countries as Spain and Ireland that has blocked the efforts to give the World Health Organization, and other United Nations agencies, a clear and general mandate to work in the birth-prevention field. A number of individual countries, however, including the United States, Britain, Sweden, and Japan, include family planning in their overseas aid programs.[37]

The world-wide acceptance of the Declaration on Population shows that the drive to limit population goes on as strongly as ever, despite the diminished evidence in support of it. But one can detect a subtle shift in recent emphasis, from birth control as a last-ditch measure to stem the population tide, to birth control as a high personal right, to be exercised for its own sake, regardless of the presence or absence of a population explosion in the world or in the practitioner's own family. The rhetoric about starving children in a crowded world is still used. And it should be used in discussing particular instances of overcrowding in certain areas as well as in formulating constructive programs to multiply our bread. But the rampant increase of contraception cannot be attributed to a solemn conviction on the part of individual men and women that they ought to do their bit to prevent the overcrowding of the earth. Rather, for the first time in history, science has given man the power to plan his offspring with virtual infallibility. More importantly, it has given him the power to take the physical pleasures of sex without running the risk of responsibilities. There are not many people who will forgo such a good thing merely because the population crisis is not as bad as it was cracked up to be. And for justification, what could be better than the lofty theory that contraception is a basic human right?

One measure of the lengths to which people will go to avoid their responsibility while enjoying unfettered sex is the popularity of the contraceptive pill. There are significant dangers involved in the use of the pill, but in the headlong rush toward the mecca of carefree sex those dangers are brushed aside and hardly discussed. As Dr. David B. Clark, professor of neurology at the University of Kentucky, put it, oral contraceptives have acquired "a diplomatic immunity from criticism" because of their social and psychological importance.[38] Dr. Herbert Ratner predicted in 1967 that the birth control pills "will be one of the major scandals of the future. It's a scandal now. No drug has had the diplomatic immunity of the pill." Dr. Ratner continued:

> The pill could not possibly have gotten on the market with what we know today. Early studies tested its effectiveness; there were no adequate studies on safety. It was introduced as "natural"; very few women understand the grave risk they're taking.[39]

The birth control pill, as introduced in 1960, contains two synthetic hormones, estrogen and progestin, that mimic the hormones produced by a pregnant woman. The synthetic hormones prevent the woman's ovaries from releasing eggs, so that a real pregnancy cannot occur.[40] Several modifications have since been devised. One involves the injection or implantation of artificial hormones in amounts large enough to work for months or even years. The ordinary pill, on the contrary, must be taken according to schedule in order to be effective and this presents a problem among uneducated women.[41]

The most serious risks from the contraceptive pill appear to be thrombophlebitis—inflammation and blood clot formation in the veins—and thromboembolism, which occurs when a blood clot or thrombus breaks loose from its original site of formation in the body and lodges elsewhere. When such a traveling clot lodges in the heart, lungs, or brain and obstructs a major blood vessel the result can be fatal. The United States Food and Drug Administration now requires labels and advertisements for contraceptive pills to state that a statistically significant association has been demonstrated between the use of oral contraceptives and thrombophlebitis and pulmonary embolism. The caution requirement was imposed after the publication in 1968 of a British study showing that the risk of death from a blood clot reaching the lungs (pulmonary embolism) or less frequently the brain (cerebral thrombosis) is at least seven or eight times higher in women using oral contraceptives than in comparable women who do not.[42] Earlier, two British neurologists, Drs. Edwin R. Bickerstaff and J. MacDonald Holmes, wrote in the *British Medical Journal* in 1967 that "there is an apparent association" between oral contraceptives and subsequent disabling strokes. The authors urged that "every care . . . be taken to try to avoid prescribing the pill for women who might offer a potential risk within the range of our very limited knowledge."[43] Three neurologists on the staff of Western Reserve University School of Medicine in Cleveland, Ohio, also found an increase of migraine headaches and strokes associated with the taking of the pill:

> During the past two years nine women between the ages of 23 and 45, patients at the University Medical Center, developed brain damage ranging from temporary impairment of vision or speech and numbness of a hand or leg, to permanent, one-sided paralysis and speech difficulties; all of which were associated in these patients with continued use of the birth control pill. A number of different brands was involved. All nine cases had previously had the warning signal of migraine headaches.[44]

In April 1967 a subcommittee of the Medical Research Council in England reported that "the sum of evidence . . . is so strong that there can be no doubt that some types of thromboembolic disorder are associated with the use of oral contraceptives."[45] There is also reason to believe that contraception may cause infertility after the use of the pills is discontinued.[46] Speaking at the 1967 meeting of the American Association of Planned Parenthood Physicians, U. S. Food and Drug Commissioner James Goddard, M.D., said that the side effects of oral contraceptives are "grossly under-reported." He called the lack of information about the contraceptive drugs a "grave issue" and stressed that "many physicians have not yet become alert to all the side effects of contraceptives."[47]

Some contraceptive pills operate by inhibiting ovulation. Thus they prevent the release of the female's egg so that it is never fertilized. But some pills do not inhibit ovulation. Rather they permit fertilization of the egg in at least some cases and then they either directly abort the fertilized egg prior to implantation or they prevent implantation, thereby preventing survival of the fertilized egg. The fact that certain so-called contraceptive pills operate by causing the destruction of the fertilized egg brings us forcefully back to the question of when human life begins. Some claim that human life begins at an arbitrarily selected point after fertilization, such as the moment of implantation. But this theory is unsupported by scientific evidence. The recently acquired popularity of the theory may be accounted for by the desire to mitigate objections to contraceptive pills that are truly abortifacient. On the contrary, any agent that terminates a pregnancy after fertilization of the egg can only be reasonably regarded as an abortifacient. And this includes at least some versions of the pill. As the U. S. Department of Health, Education, and Welfare reported in its 1962 Survey of Research on Reproduction Related to Birth and Population Control:

> All of the measures which impair the viability of the zygote at any time between the instant of fertilization and the completion of labor constitute, in the strict sense, procedures for inducing abortion.[48]

Intrauterine devices are another effective means of birth prevention. They are small loops, usually plastic, that are inserted into a patient's uterus. The cost of the device is very small, and it usually requires little, if any, attention. It is estimated that between 6 million and 8 million women have been fitted with IUDs, roughly half the number taking the pill. About 1 million American women are believed to be using the IUD.[49] The IUD is not quite as reliable as the pill but both are more effective than other forms of contraception.[50] The IUD, however, does carry a small risk of infection and uterine perforation. The Food and Drug Administration in 1968 cited four American cases in which fatal infections occurred after the devices were put into place. The report indicated there was a causal relationship between the infections and the deaths.[51]

It is commonly agreed that the IUD does not interfere with ovulation or conception. Rather, it appears likely that it prevents the implantation that normally follows conception. Dr. Earl L. Parr of Rockefeller University in New York reported that animal experiments he has done indicate that the IUD operates by killing fertilized ova before they can become implanted.[52] If this is true, the IUD is not a contraceptive at all but rather, like some of the pills, causes an abortion and thereby kills an existing human being. Nevertheless, the popularity of the IUD and the pill is undiminished by such considerations.

It is significant, too, that even Catholics are weakening in this Age of the Pill. According to a 1965 survey of 5600 married American women, 84% said they have used contraception and 6% more said they expect to use it. The sociologists who conducted the study concluded that more than half of American white Catholic married women say they have used a birth control method other than rhythm, a quarter have used rhythm only, and slightly less than one quarter have used no method. In the researcher's opinion, "the fact of being Catholic is becoming less significant as a factor in shaping attitudes toward fertility control and in the practice of contraception itself."[53] This lessening of religious strictures against contraception is not limited to the United States. At the 1967 conference of the International Planned Parenthood Federation in Santiago, Chile, it was estimated that at least 1.5 million women in predominantly Catholic Latin America are using the contraceptive pill. A twenty-seven-year-old Chilean woman attended a class reunion at the Roman Catholic Sacred Heart College in Santiago and reported:

> There were about 30 members of my class there, nearly all married and attractive, but none was pregnant. Five years ago many of them had a baby on the way or just home from the hospital. It suddenly dawned on me that they were all on the pill.[54]

The general Catholic principles on contraception were stated by Pope Pius XII:

> Our predecessor, Pius XI, of happy memory, in his encyclical *Casti Connubii*, December 31, 1930, solemnly proclaimed anew the fundamental law governing the marital act and conjugal relations: that any attempt on the part of married people to deprive this act of its inherent force and to impede the procreation of new life, either in the performance of the act itself or in the course of development of its natural consequences, is immoral; and no alleged "indication" or need can convert an intrinsically immoral act into a moral and lawful one.
>
> This precept is as valid today as it was yesterday; and it will be the same

tomorrow and always, because it does not imply a precept of human law but is the expression of a law that is natural and divine.[55]

When Pope Paul VI commented on the further study he was then giving to the question in light of the problems raised by the pill, he emphasized:

As we have already stated . . . the norm until now taught by the Church, integrated by wise instructions of the Council, demands faithful and generous observance. It cannot be considered not binding as if the magisterium of the Church were in a state of doubt at the present time, whereas it is in a moment of study and reflection concerning matters which have been put before it as worthy of the most attentive consideration.[56]

Finally, on July 29, 1968, Pope Paul, in his encyclical, *Humanae Vitae,* flatly condemned all forms of artificial contraception. The ban extended to "every action which, either in anticipation of the conjugal act or in its accomplishment, or in the development of its natural consequences, proposes, whether as an end or as a means, to render procreation impossible."[57]

This is not a treatise on Catholic moral theology. However, the strength of the contraceptive movement can be seen in the way it carried Catholics along, before this new encyclical, despite the adamant though generalized prohibitions of the Church. Moreover, so strong is the tide that even the Pope's unequivocal condemnation of the pill, the IUD, and other contraceptive refinements may be unable to curb the indulgence of Catholics in the irresponsible spirit of the day. Also, the Catholic disintegration has been hastened by some intellectuals within the camp. Applying the destructive theories of situation ethics,[58] they advocate contraception in a way that is demonstrably out of harmony with the view proclaimed by the authoritative magisterium of the Church. It may be appropriate here to recall Cardinal Newman's comment: "It is a miserable time when a man's Catholic profession is no voucher for his orthodoxy, and when a teacher of religion may be within the Church's pale, yet external to her faith."[59] More to the point on the subject of contraception, G. K. Chesterton regarded it as a pre-eminent moral evil. And when the Anglican Lambeth Conference of 1930 weakened the prohibition against contraception, Chesterton's reaction was worth remembering today:

My concern is . . . with all to whom I might once have looked to defend the country of the Christian altars. They ought surely to know that the foe now on the frontiers offers no terms of compromise; but threatens a complete destruction. And they have sold the pass.[60]

The Future

The real danger in America today is not the population explosion but the copulation explosion. As Dr. Mary Calderone, executive director of the Sex Information and Education Council of the United States, says: "We're seeing an explosion of sexual expression. It's not necessarily the in-bed expression, but in all our communications media—in all our waking thoughts, waking music, waking reading, there's this tremendous explosion, almost an obsession with sex. The *genital* aspects of sex."[61] In his famous essay "Down with Sex!" England's Malcolm Muggeridge observes that Americans have made erotica "a mania, a sickness."[62] The sickness attacks the young with destructive force. Teenagers and young adults under twenty-five account for over 50% of the total reported cases of infectious syphilis. Venereal diseases infect more than 250,000 young people annually. Gonorrhea is the most prevalent venereal disease in the ten-to-nineteen-year age group; syphilis is second. At present the fifteen-to-nineteen age group has a reported rate of infection of both gonorrhea and infectious syphilis more than double that of all other age groups.[63] Illegitimate births in this country have tripled in number in the past twenty-five years. Forty per cent of the unwed mothers are fifteen to nineteen years of age.[64] We appear to be emulating other countries that are reaping a whirlwind from their relaxation of sexual standards. In Denmark, for example, "the registered maternal ranks of sub-18-year olds swelled from 569 in 1940 to 2,198 in 1964. In the latter years, 79 women who gave birth were age 15, 500 were 16, and 1,619 were 17. Unmarried mothers in recent years contributed about one of every 10 live births, 40 of 100 brides are already pregnant."[65] The situation in Denmark is not unique. In Sweden the number of unmarried mothers is increasing and one in three brides is pregnant on her wedding day. In 1966 a Danish "pregnancy hygiene" law was enacted, authorizing any fifteen-to-eighteen-year-old girl to go to a physician or birth control clinic to be fitted with a diaphragm or to get instruction in other contraceptive methods. This law operates irrespective of parental consent.[66] That same year, Katherine B. Oettinger, chief of the Children's Bureau of the Department of Health, Education, and Welfare, indicated family planning services in the United States "would be available to all who request them."[67] It is reported that prescriptions for contraceptive pills are available to students through 45% of the nation's college health services. A survey of 315 member institutions of the American College Health Association revealed, however, that at present only one in twenty-five prescribed the pills for single women who do not intend to marry in the near future.[68] Mount Sinai Hospital in New York City conducts an Adolescent Clinic where, with the blessing of the city's Health Department, unmarried girls between the ages of thirteen and sixteen are issued contraceptive pills if they are deemed to be "sexually active."[69] Incidentally, the Food and Drug Administration has warned that giving birth control pills to girls whose bone growth is not complete can tend to bring about bone closure, permanently stunting the future growth of the bones.[70]

The nearly universal practice of contraception is at once both cause and effect. It is a cause of the breakdown of morality in this country and it is also an effect of a deeper malady, the headlong and selfish flight from responsibility.

Contraception is an obvious cause of the copulation explosion. It removes the fear of pregnancy and thereby facilitates all manner of youthful experiments, "arrangements" between college students, and adulteries by married persons. Too little attention has been paid to the obvious connection between easy contraception and easy morals among the unmarried and the married as well. The issue of contraception is basic to the problems of life and death discussed in this book. As a matter of fact it is the most elemental and the most determinative issue in the book. It was not without reason that one commentator remarked:

> The works of the scientific humanists are there to prove that man's attitude to contraception determines whether he will think it wrong or right for a mother to kill her defective child, or for a doctor "gently and humanely to extinguish his patient's life."[71]

Contraception, however, is also an effect of the current flight from responsibility. This is a secularized society. We have lost sight of God. We have turned away not only from a transcendent commitment to a Creator but also from any firm commitment to others. The standard of conduct is increasingly our own individual convenience and our own pleasure.

One reason why contraception has risen so high is that respect for life has fallen so low. The philosophy of unrestraint is in the ascendant, and the pursuit of pleasure is not to be impeded by considerations of ethics or the welfare of others. In truth, the birth control fever and the underlying sickness of irresponsibility nourish each other. The spiral goes on, out of hand, to the point where the only recourse can be repression if society is to survive:

> Birth control *mores* create a mentality of "unwanting" babies. Furthermore, it is not a practice only but a new philosophy of man and sex, a new "way of life." It means the abandonment of self-control over sexual urges; it implicitly authorizes sexual promiscuity. The real problem of our time is that society tolerates a continuous and ubiquitous display, by every medium of mass communication, of artificial libidinous solicitation, which makes it unnaturally difficult for people, particularly young people, to be continent; and then offers a remedy, contraceptives, which merely increases the incontinence. Promiscuity is the logic of birth control; but to have promiscuity with impunity there must also be abortion and infanticide, sterilization and euthanasia. The logical contraceptionist must insist that if these cannot be generalized by persuasion, they must be imposed by law. It has long been recognized that there is a connection between eroticism and totalitarianism.[72]

It is not surprising that the copulation explosion leads to repression. Modern science has given man power to control life itself and to fornicate with material impunity. This power, if unchecked, can destroy society. That it should be checked by self-control is, simply, ordained by the natural law. But if that internal check, which demands an exercise of personal responsibility, is not accepted, then an external control must be imposed. Thus it was that Dr. Lincoln H. Day, Yale University demographer, said, "Reproduction is a private act, but it is not a private affair. It has far-reaching social consequences." He said that no one, regardless of wealth, had the right to have more than two or three children. He is, incidentally, the father of two children.[73] In a similar direction, Professor Kingsley Davis of the University of California at Berkeley has suggested that "family planning" is not effective as a long-term method of population control since it leaves too much initiative and choice up to the individual husband and wife. Professor Davis disputed whether such planning programs had any real effect on the ground that nations undergoing rapid economic development, such as Taiwan and South Korea, usually experienced a decline in the birth rate anyway. He said that reproduction should be regulated according to a rational plan for the benefit of society rather than according to the differing plans of the various families. According to Professor Davis, the "next step" is to de-emphasize the family and discourage child-bearing by such devices as postponing marriages, imposing a child tax, stopping the taxing of single persons more than married ones, aborting illegitimate pregnancies at government expense, charging a substantial fee for marriage licenses, reducing paid maternity leaves and paying people who volunteer to be sterilized.[74]

In 1967, Secretary of Interior Stewart Udall told a Planned Parenthood meeting in Denver that the time had come for the federal government to establish "optimum population levels" and to impose tax penalties on couples who have large families.[75] A similar attitude toward children was revealed by Dr. Mary S. Calderone when she complained: "We have yet to beat our public health drums for birth control in the way we beat them for polio vaccine; we are still unable to put babies in the class of dangerous epidemics, even though this is the exact truth."[76]

Government coercion in the area of family planning is not entirely a vision of the future. In some ways it is already a fact for recipients of government subsidies. Increasingly, for example, welfare case workers are pressing their clients to accept the advantages of "family planning." Some Negro spokesmen, including Cecil Moore, NAACP leader of Philadelphia, have claimed that government efforts in this area are really designed to reduce the Negro population.[77] The Roman Catholic bishops of the United States in 1966 criticized government welfare agencies for invading the privacy of welfare clients and coercing them into practicing contraception:

> Far from merely seeking to provide information in response to requests from the needy, government activities increasingly seek aggressively to persuade and even coerce the underprivileged to practice birth control. In this, government

far exceeds its proper role. The citizens's right to decide without pressure is now threatened.[78]

Implicit coercion, however, is inherent when government provides birth control assistance to welfare recipients. The same tendency operates in private relations between doctor and patient. Dr. Allan C. Barnes of Johns Hopkins Hospital emphasized this point:

> We say that we'll let the patient choose—but who's fooling whom? The way we present this to the patient not infrequently stacks the selection, and her choice is heavily influenced. We are not letting the patient choose as much as we innocently disclaim we are.
>
> We're pushing our patients, and our practice ends up matching us. . . . This "I would let the patient choose" is an innocent phrase to use, but in the long run, we push an opinion on people psychologically more than we realize.[79]

Indeed, the coercive potential in this area extends far beyond the mere limitation of births. Scientists will soon have the power to practice human engineering on a scale heretofore reserved to science fiction. Mass administration of contraceptives through food and water supplies, with fertility-creating antidotes supplied to those licensed by the state to bear children, was suggested in 1963 by Dr. F. H. C. Crick of the Medical Research Council Laboratory for Molecular Biology in England. His argument has to be seen to be believed but we disregard it at our peril:

> Do people have the right to have children at all? It would not be very difficult for a government to put something into our food so that nobody should have children. Then possibly—and this is hypothetical—they could provide another chemical that would reverse the effect of the first, and only people licensed to bear children would be given this second chemical. This isn't so wild that we need not discuss it. Is it the general feeling that people do have the right to have children? This is taken for granted because it is part of Christian ethics, but in terms of humanist ethics I do not see why people should have the right to have children. I think that if we can get across to people the idea that their children are not entirely their own business and that it is not a private matter, it would be an enormous step forward. If one did have a licensing scheme, the first child might be admitted on rather easy terms. If the parents were genetically unfavorable, they might be allowed to have only one child, or possibly two under certain special circumstances. That seems to me the sort of practical problem that is raised by our new knowledge of biology. . . . The type of solution which might become socially acceptable is simply to encourage by financial means those people who are more socially

desirable to have more children. The obvious way to do this is to tax children. This seems dreadful to a good liberal because it is exactly the opposite of everything he has been brought up to believe. But at least it is logical. There are various objections: There will be people who, however much the tax, will have many children, but they may be a minority.[80]

A similar idea, including also contraceptive inoculation, was advanced at a 1964 symposium by Dr. Joseph W. Goldzieher, a pioneer in the development of synthetic hormonal conception control:

> The immunication technics are eminently practical in this respect, particularly if passive immunity of suitable duration can be induced with single injections. Compulsory "vaccination" may be a difficult procedure requiring much organization and expense, but it can be made to work, and the necessary know-how is at hand.
>
> One must also think of methods whereby a population could be exposed to antifertility agents distributed in a dietary staple, just as salt is iodized or water is fluoridated. . . .
>
> In this way, it would finally be possible to shift the burden of responsibility for propagation on people who exercise their desire to multiply by a simple act of free will, that of obtaining the necessary antidote at such time as they wish to resume fertility. If such an antidote were freely available to all, there could be no ethical objection to the chemical sterilization of entire populations. Indeed, for the first time since sexual reproduction began, propagation would be the result of a positive act of free will. Ethically and sociologically, no higher goal could be attained.[81]

Dr. Allan C. Barnes of Johns Hopkins University commented favorably on these ideas and went on to prove that some doctors tend to endow themselves with the omniscience of God Almighty:

> Another version of my brave new world has a soluble antiovulation medication in our drinking water. Every tap that runs, every public drinking fountain carries it.
>
> In such a society, one will issue to the medical profession bottles of drinking water that are nonmedicated. I will not yield this to the priests, I will not yield this to the state liquor store, I will keep this in the hands of the medical profession which will give us another thing that we need in our social development, a greater use of the preconception examination; preconception counseling and patient-education on the pattern of behavior in very early pregnancy.
>
> . . . This is not too bad a society to contemplate, particularly so if this mythical chemical turns out to have a pleasant taste![82]

More recently, Dr. A. W. Andison of Winnipeg, Canada, predicted the development of an effective, inexpensive, intravaginal device that would be inserted in all young girls and removed only when pregnancy is desired. This automatic contraception, said the doctor, would mean that "Women would be free from unwanted pregnancy, every child would be a wanted child and there would be no more illegitimate babies."[83] Another type of proposed contraceptive drug involves the insertion under the skin of tiny pellets that would constantly release into the blood stream a sufficient amount of a synthetic hormone, progestin, to prevent pregnancy for three months or more.[84] Successful tests have been conducted with the "morning-after" birth control pill. This prevents the implantation of the ovum, which occurs on the sixth or seventh day following fertilization, and therefore it must be taken within that period of time after intercourse.[85] The "morning-after" pill clearly causes an abortion. But it also poses the moral issue inescapably. These refinements of the birth control art ensure that personal decisions for or against fornication and adultery will soon be moral judgments uninfluenced by possible fear of pregnancy.

It is easy to point with alarm to the potential abuse of the newly found powers to control reproduction. Even more startling examples were covered in Chapter II, dealing with artificial insemination. However, it is more important to formulate an alternative policy. In short, government must act upon a coherent judgment as to the civic legitimacy of contraception itself.

For one thing, contraception can properly be described as a perversion. It would seem to fit Sigmund Freud's description:

It is a characteristic common to all the perversions that in them reproduction as an aim is put aside. This is actually the criterion by which we judge whether a sexual activity is perverse—if it departs from reproduction in its aims and pursues the attainment of gratification independently. You will understand therefore that the gulf and turning-point in the development of the sexual life lies at the point of its subordination to the purposes of reproduction. Everything that occurs before this conversion takes place, and everything which refuses to conform to it and serves the pursuit of gratification alone, is called by the unhonoured title of "perversion" and as such is despised.[86]

Contraception used to be denounced as race suicide. Although we must beware of overdramatizing, it is fair to call it just that. But race suicide here does not refer merely to reduction in numbers.

It is true that births in Sweden, Norway, Japan, England, and France are already only barely sufficient, if that, to replenish the population. And the United States, initially for its white population and ultimately for its Negroes too, is nearing that point in the downward slide of its birth rate.[87] But in a more profound sense, unrestrained birth control portends the suicide of the race. The basic unit of civilized society is the family. As Rabbi Pesach Z. Levovitz, president of the Rabbinical Council of America, says, "The family is the basic unit of communal and religious life and the training ground for our future generations."[88] The pervasive practice of contraception, with its promotion of promiscuity and its weakening of responsibility, is destructive of family life. No society can long survive unless promiscuity is restrained or at least discouraged and unless a solid family life is promoted. We could learn much in this respect from the Soviet Union. The leaders of that Communist nation abandoned their earlier permissiveness in 1949 and returned to a strict code in sexual matters, as indicated in these excerpts from the journal, *Soviet Education:*

> The October [1917] socialist revolution wiped out the political, legal and economic inequality of women, but some people have incorrectly understood this freedom and have decided that human sex life can be carried on with a disorderly succession of husbands and wives.
>
> In a tightly organized society, a socialistic society, such practices necessarily lead to a laxity and vulgarization of relationships unworthy of man, cause difficult personality problems, unhappiness and disruption of the family, making orphans of the children.
>
> Every parent must work toward training the future citizen to be happy only in family love and to seek the joys of sex life only in marriage. If parents do not set such a goal for themselves and do not reach it, their children will lead a promiscuous sex life full of dramas, unhappiness, misery and injury to society.[89]

We, too, stand in need of a public policy committed to promote the family and chastity. The chastity to which this refers is not synonymous with virginity or sexual abstinence. It is, rather, what Pope Paul VI called the "mastery of the spirit over the flesh." As he further said:

> This mastery is essential to human dignity. It is part of the virtue which the ancients call temperance and which is nothing other than self-possession. I dare say that chastity obtains something that people of today value highly,

and rightly: freedom, autonomy, liberty. Do not let us be afraid to say out loud what most men think to themselves: there is no true liberty without the spirit of chastity.[90]

Malcolm Muggeridge recently resigned as rector of the University of Edinburgh in protest over the student council demands that the university provide free contraceptive pills for women students. In his resignation address, he spoke on behalf of a lost virtue:

> One of the Beatitudes has never quite impressed me so much before—Blessed Are the Pure at Heart for They Shall See God. . . .
>
> To see God—that is the highest preoccupation of the human spirit.
>
> Seeing God means understanding. It should be the essential quest of universities like this one and their students and their staff. The achievement of this quest is not through sensations, however generated, or success. . . . I never yet met a man made happy by sensual acts alone, still less by stupefication of drugs and alcohol.[91]

The law is not merely a repressive agent but can be an educative force. The solidity of the family should be a principal end of our domestic policy. The function of the law here is broader than merely requiring marriage licenses and imposing restrictions, however minimal, on divorce. Rather the law must come to grips with contraception. "Contraception is the sister of abortion, the handmaiden of divorce and the companion of sexual license and venereal disease," as Bishop Alden J. Bell of Sacramento put it. If the government continues to encourage contraception, it will contribute to the continued disintegration of the family. Perhaps Dr. Herbert Ratner put his finger on one cause when he said:

> The moment you separate the recreational from the procreational aspect of sex, you are cut off from the kind of love that has fidelity behind it. The worst thing is that sex becomes very boring, so people turn to drugs and the search for thrills which can't offer the deepseated emotional satisfactions they need.[92]

Government cannot be the keeper of the people's conscience on all things. Furthermore, the role of government in prohibiting immoral conduct is quite limited. But the role does exist. It is a truism that not everything that is immoral should be illegal. But it is the other side of the coin that some immoral things should be made illegal where it is reasonably necessary for the common good. Thomas Aquinas described the principle this way:

Human law is enacted for the community in general, and in the community the majority are not perfected in virtue. Therefore, human law does not prohibit all the vices which those of special virtue avoid, but only the more serious vices, which the majority of people, with ordinary virtue, can avoid; and especially those vices which injure the common good and whose prohibition is necessary for the preservation of society.

Human law aims to lead men to virtue, not all at once, but gradually. Therefore, it does not require of the average imperfect man the standard of perfection attained by the virtuous; i.e., it does not prohibit everything that is sinful. If it did, the average imperfect man, unable to observe the law's requirements, might fall into complete lawlessness. . . . The laws would come to be despised and, through contempt of law, men might become more depraved than ever.[93]

There is, in short, a proper though limited role for the law in this area. The first thing that government at all levels should do is to stop subsidizing contraception. Teenagers, as well as adults for that matter, should not be given contraceptive assistance by public agencies. In Prince George's County, Maryland, a suburb of Washington, D.C., unwed mothers were denied welfare payments until they had taken a course in birth prevention and had been issued a Certificate of Instruction in Life Prevention.[94] Similar requirements were enforced in other communities until the federal government ruled that the instruction could not be compulsory. However, any government instruction here is doubly wrong. It promotes contraception when it should be discouraged. And it tends to degenerate into an implicit compulsion of individuals to conform. But the vice here is not merely the implicit coercion. It is the government participation itself. Government should not even be neutral toward contraception. Rather it should actively discourage it and should not provide contraceptive assistance even to those who voluntarily request it.

Secondly, government should strictly forbid the sale, or other provision, of contraceptive devices, including pills, to unmarried persons under twenty-one. The use of such materials, as distinguished from their sale, whether by married persons or others, could not be prohibited without an obvious invasion of privacy.[95] A number of states already restrict the sale, advertising, or distribution of contraceptives, including prohibitions against the public advertising or offering of contraceptive materials, and some require that they be available for sale only on a doctor's prescription.[96] These laws, applicable to adults as well as minors, are sound in principle. But to a great extent they are dormant and their full enforcement may not be readily attainable as a matter of practicality. However, an immediately realistic and practical case can be made for prohibiting the sale or other provision of contraceptive devices to unmarried minors. We routinely forbid the sale or giving of alcoholic beverages to minors, except by their parents in private, and there is no sound reason why a similar prohibition could not be effectively extended to contraceptives. At the very least, a prohibition of this sort would end the dispensation of contraceptives to students by some college administrations.

Thirdly, and more importantly, government should actively undertake to dissuade teenagers from premarital sexual intercourse. The goal should be not a false objectivity that refuses to make the necessary value judgment, but a frank effort to convince them. They have to be convinced how profoundly wrong was the president of the student council at a New York City high school when she said: "From all my reading, I know there's nothing more beautiful than the unification of two people who are right for each other. I don't see what a little piece of paper has to do with it."[97] Government should encourage a more sensible attitude. For example, realistic controls are needed on the dissemination of pornography, particularly to the young. And these controls can be imposed consistently with a reasoned interpretation of freedom of speech. At the same time, a shift in the official approach is needed, toward a constructive promotion of chastity and respect for marriage.

Some will object that these proposals involve government in the enforcement of morality and probably in an invasion of the free exercise of religion through the coercive imposition of what are basically Christian tenets. However, we are primarily suggesting government encouragement, not enforcement, of morality. As to the religious-freedom argument, we might well recall the comment of Monsignor George A. Kelly, then of the Family Life Bureau of the Archdiocese of New York, that "People who believe that an iron wall must separate church and state so that no state money may subsidize the teaching of monogamy or chastity are perfectly happy at departments of welfare subsidizing fornication and adultery."[98]

To the extent that these proposals involve government prohibitions rather than mere encouragement, they are limited in their scope and are justified by the necessity of promoting the common good. Government ought to discourage contraception, not because it is sinful, according to the edict of any particular religion, but because it poses a clear and present danger to the endurance of the family as the basic unit of society. A policy of this sort would cease to treat contraception as a neutral phenomenon. It is not. It is dangerous and it ought to be discouraged and restrained to the extent that we can do so without an undue invasion of privacy.

Similarly, adultery and fornication are not merely neutral acts, although the prevailing relativism tends to regard them as morally indifferent in themselves. The dean of students at Fordham University has said that he would urge any of his students cohabiting together without benefit of marriage to "change their pattern of living. But," he added, "we'd do the same to any group of fellows who were caught playing their record player too loud early in the morning."[99] If we cannot make an operative distinction between intercourse and a phonograph, perhaps it tells us something about our society. On the contrary, adultery and fornication should be recognized as inimical to the promotion of the family. A sound public policy ought to penalize them both. Adultery is sexual intercourse where at least one of the parties is married to someone else. Fornication is sexual intercourse between unmarried persons. Either one is destructive of family integrity. The destruction is direct and immediate in the case of adultery. Fornication is indirect in its effect, but it is no less harmful. This is particularly so when the act is performed by teenagers who will shortly assume the responsibilities of family and children but who cannot be expected to discard overnight a habit of sexual license acquired during the teen years. One cannot envision an enduring family unit in a society in which the act of sexual intercourse is not, as a matter of principle and policy, reserved to the marital relation. To the furthest extent compatible with competing liberties, the law ought to encourage that reservation. A criminal proscription of fornication as well as adultery, with appropriate juvenile court procedures applied in the case of minors, would serve to reinforce the family in this regard. There is no competing interest in marital privacy involved here, since the partners in adultery or fornication are not married to each other. Nor would the penalty be precluded by the same considerations that lead us to conclude that the use, as distinguished from the sale, of contraceptives ought not to be forbidden in any case. There is a significant difference, in degree of intrusion upon privacy and in delicacy of proof, in determining, on the one hand, whether an act of intercourse has taken place and, on the other hand, how it was performed. As a practical matter, an effective restriction on the sale of contraceptives, at least to unmarried minors, would greatly reduce the incidence of promiscuity without any vigorous prosecution of adultery or fornication. The latter acts, however, should be prohibited by the law as a matter of principle and as an auxiliary means of discouraging promiscuity.

In short, the law should actively encourage chastity, in the general sense, and should discourage contraception by dissuasion and, where appropriate, by limited legal prohibitions. And let us hope that the public attitude will follow suit. For the unrestrained practice of contraception is harmful to society. It offers an obvious inducement to promiscuity, liberating the user from the possible consequences of his act. It thus promotes the irresponsibility from which we suffer today. Even in the married state, this irresponsibility is evident. Nor can contraception be justified by any of the arguments commonly advanced in its behalf. The world population explosion is neither so serious nor so widespread as we are sometimes told. Even if it were, it could not justify the indulgence in the practice by the American middle class. In this country and elsewhere, welfare recipients and poor people have to be bribed or coerced into using contraceptives or undergoing sterilization. But the pill and other contraceptive refinements are quite the rage, in certain quarters of the middle and upper income brackets in this country. The poor of this world, it would seem, have more sense than those who, by reason of superior education, ought to be more perceptive.

Contraception has become a way of life for many. So has irresponsibility, and the two are not unrelated. Some Americans, who are rich as Croesus compared to the swarming peasants of Pakistan, justify their practice of contraception as necessary to provide their children with the practical necessities of American life. But the difficulty here lies in the definition of a necessity. It is literally true that many children in this land are "under-deprived," that their parents have bestowed, or inflicted, on them a surfeit of material and status adornments, from dancing classes to country club memberships to the late-model cars jamming our high school parking lots. Often, material largesse is employed as an unthinking substitute for parental love and care. As columnist Jim Bishop once said, when the children are small the parental attitude is too often, "Give the kid a wind-up toy and let's get the hell out of here." When the child grows up, we cannot be too surprised when his attitude is, "Give Mom a kiss and let's go crack that gas station."

This is not to disparage the condition of those who are really in need. In America today a family can be in need even with a substantial income. A combination of taxes, child-rearing and other living costs can cause genuine financial difficulty. It is not entirely in jest that some claim that the forgotten Americans are those who are too wealthy to benefit from welfare handouts and too poor not to be hurt by the crushing burden of taxes and inflation. But contraception should be discouraged as a remedy for those in need. As unlikely as it sounds in a day of indulgence, the idea of self-control is worth suggesting as an alternative. It is likely that in most cases, where contraceptives are used by married couples today, there is neither actual need nor a potential menace to health from another pregnancy. Rather, it is too easy for married couples to blur the line between things that are desirable and those that are necessary. Worse still is the tendency to regard even undesirable things, such as inordinate material benefits, as necessities. And somehow the notion of self-control has been lost in the shuffle. Occasional periodic abstinence is rarely considered as the alternative to pregnancy. Instead, even a limited self-control is assumed to be harmful and beyond the power of ordinary people. It is no surprise, then, that children learn by example from their elders and spurn the virtue of chastity and the self-restraint it requires. The statistical results, in teen-age venereal disease, pregnancies, and confusion, are predictable and tragic. But they are avoidable and common sense should impel us to avoid them, so far as we can, by changing our direction toward an advancement of responsibility in this critical area. The essential point of this chapter is that the law and public policy, without invading the legitimate rights of privacy, should change from encouragement to discouragement of contraception. If this change in direction occurs, we can expect the practice of contraception to be reduced to manageable proportions. And we can go a long way toward restoring the lost virtue of personal responsibility in this and future generations.

8

STERILIZATION

In India sterilization is the national pastime. Government health teams travel from village to village, urging the blessings of sterilization and, not incidentally, offering two dollars as a bounty to each man in exchange for his surrender of his reproductive capacity. If another person persuades him to submit, the persuader is rewarded with forty cents. Between May and October of 1967 no fewer than 800,000 vasectomies were performed in India. The pastime has even developed its folk heroes. Dr. Bububhai S. Patel "is to vasectomies what Jack Nicklaus is to golf."[1] "The analogy" to Jack Nicklaus "may sound farfetched, but not after you have seen the two silver plaques and six loving cups Dr. Patel has garnered for his prowess in population control. The most recent award was for coming in first in vasectomies in the September fortnight with a score of 681."[2] The New York *Times* correspondent who reported the event did not mention the score of the runner-up. Presumably he was so far behind that there was no need for a playoff. Meanwhile, Dr. Patel continues on the circuit, at a fee of ninety-three cents a stroke. "At 7 rupees an operation, he was also a big money winner," the *Times* man reports.

Sterilization is a surgical operation that deprives the patient of the ability to procreate or conceive children. It does not interfere with the capacity to engage in sexual intercourse. The most common sterilization procedures are vasectomy for males and salpingectomy for females. Vasectomy involves the ligation and resection of a small part of the vas deferens, thereby preventing the passage of sperm into the seminal fluid. In salpingectomy, the Fallopian tubes between the ovaries and the womb are cut and tied. Apparently salpingectomy is irreversible. Reversal can be achieved in a minority of vasectomies, perhaps in as many as one third of the cases. Despite this problematical prospect of reversal, however, sterilization has to be regarded as practically irreversible, for purposes of coherent analysis.[3] Both vasectomy and salpingectomy are practically certain of success in achieving sterilization.[4] Vasectomy is a mere office operation. It takes less than ten minutes and the patient suffers no significant disability. Salpingectomy must be performed in a hospital and the recovery period is about one week. A vasectomy poses practically no danger to the physical health of the man who undergoes it. A salpingectomy is quite safe also, although there is a statistically slight risk of death from the operation.[5] There is some evidence, however, that sterilization can entail a significant risk of adverse psychological reactions. One recent report revealed a 15% unsatisfactory psychiatric outcome rate among sterilized women. As one British commentator concluded, "What the planners tend to forget is that material success is not necessarily synonymous with emotional satisfaction. A sterilized mother is not necessarily a contented member of the community."[6] Other studies, however, have discounted the risk of adverse psychiatric reactions. Psychiatrist Robert W. Laidlaw concluded that "Voluntary sterilization can and does contribute to mental health . . . by reducing the anxiety caused by fear of unwanted pregnancies; by preventing children from being born to irresponsible parents with resultant neglect and social ills. . . . All this can be accomplished without unfavorable psychological effects and with a high ratio of satisfaction."[7]

Sterilization can also be achieved by castration of the male so that he is incapable of performing intercourse. This renders the man impotent rather than technically sterile but the practical effect is the same. A female may be sterilized infallibly and irreversibly by surgical removal of the ovaries or by a hysterectomy in which the womb is removed. But these radical methods are far less frequently used than vasectomy and salpingectomy.

Sterilization can be either voluntary, with the consent of the patient, or involuntary, against his will. Sterilization may be performed for several purposes. It can be therapeutic, punitive, eugenic, or contraceptive. A sterilization is therapeutic when it is designed to improve bodily health, as when the womb is removed because it is diseased. Punitive sterilization is imposed as a penalty for crime.

Eugenic sterilization aims to prevent the birth of defective offspring by sterilizing those persons who would be likely to have such children. Contraceptive sterilization is not required directly for bodily health but is designed to prevent conception. The concepts of therapeutic and contraceptive sterilization merge when a pregnancy would be injurious to the health of the mother and the sterilization is designed to preserve her health by preventing conception.

Sterilization can hardly be called major surgery, in terms of the complexity of the procedure or the risk to the patient. However, it is not a tonsillectomy. It puts a man or woman permanently, for practical purposes, out of the business of reproduction. Because of its termination of a basic human capacity, it has enormous significance for the patient whether he realizes it or not and whether he wants it or not. It is in this context that its legitimacy must be determined.

Nobody today will deny that sterilization is ethically proper where it occurs as an incident of an operation to remove a diseased womb or ovaries or as a necessary incident of any other operation required to promote directly the health of the body. This is the essential meaning of therapeutic sterilization. The operative ethical principle is the double effect. The parts of the body exist for the welfare of the whole and where a diseased womb, appendix, or arm threatens the entire body, the offending organ or limb can ethically be removed. In performing the operation, say to remove the womb, the intent is to remove a diseased organ, not to achieve sterilization. The sterilization is an unavoidable and necessary incident of the performance of the legitimate operation to remove the womb. The law does not restrict or forbid the performance of therapeutic sterilizations of this sort, where the sterilization occurs as an incident of a surgically justified operation to preserve the health of the body.

Legal and ethical problems do arise when sterilization is employed as a punitive, eugenic, or contraceptive measure. Analytically, we can treat them separately but each can be fully understood only in context with the others. Indeed it frequently happens that a particular sterilization involves all three elements, the punitive, the eugenic, and the contraceptive. A case in point is that of Mrs. Nancy Hernandez. She was living in Santa Barbara, California, with Joe

Sanchez when she was arrested on April 14, 1966, in a drive against marijuana users. Joe was not her husband but was the father of her second child, three months old. Mrs. Hernandez pleaded guilty to a charge of being found in a place where marijuana was being used. It was her first offense. In passing sentence on her, Municipal Court Judge Frank P. Kearney expressed his concern over her two children and any more she might have in the future. He then sentenced her to six months in jail, but offered her a release on probation if she would agree to a sterilization operation.

Mrs. Hernandez, a recipient of public assistance under the county welfare program, agreed to the bargain. Later, however, she changed her mind and refused to undergo the sterilization. On her appeal, the appellate court overruled the lower court and put her on an ordinary probation. The appellate judge ruled that Judge Kearney had acted arbitrarily and in excess of his power in conditioning probation upon the performance of a sterilization.[8] He had attempted to compel sterilization in a way that was partly punitive, partly eugenic, and partly contraceptive and he was unauthorized to do so by any governing statute.

Thirteen states have statutes providing for the sterilization of criminals.[9] Danish law permits the castration of sexual offenders, but no American states authorize it.[10] Criminal sterilization statutes are partly eugenic in their purpose. But they are also and essentially penal. As such, they require us to consider the power of the state to impose sterilization as a punishment for crime. If we concede the right of the state to impose capital punishment in an appropriate case, it is difficult to see how we can deny in theory its power to deprive the criminal not of his (or her) life but of a faculty of which he might be just as glad to be relieved. However, there are complicating factors.

If sterilization is urged as a means to reduce crime by preventing the criminal from having offspring, it is eugenic sterilization. If the sterilization is designed rather to prevent the commission of further crimes by the person sterilized or by other persons, who would be deterred by the prospect of sterilization, it is basically punitive. Most if not all of the punitive sterilization laws are at least partly eugenic in their motivation. They single out convicted criminals for sterilization but they appear to do so for the assumed reason that preventing those criminals from propagating will prevent the generation of future criminals. The eugenic overtones seem predominant when the sterilization is limited to repeated offenders or those defined as habitual criminals. When a law subjects certain types of criminals to sterilization, it may be open to objection on the ground that the classification is unreasonable. It may be arbitrary to single out those criminals and penalize them alone with the loss of their reproductive capacity. In legal terms, it may deprive them of the equal protection of the laws. The Fourteenth Amendment to the United States Constitution provides that "No State shall . . . deny to any person within its jurisdiction the equal protection of the laws." A similar prohibition implicitly binds the federal government. Generally a statute denies equal protection of the laws if the classification it makes is arbitrary, capricious, or unreasonable. The Supreme Court of the United States, in Skinner v. Oklahoma, in 1942, unanimously invalidated an Oklahoma statute authorizing the compulsory sterilization of habitual criminals convicted of "felonies involving moral turpitude." Jack T. Skinner was convicted in 1926 for stealing chickens and was sentenced to the Oklahoma State Reformatory. In 1929 he was convicted of armed robbery and was again sentenced to the reformatory. He was still confined there when, in 1935, the legislature passed the Oklahoma Habitual Criminal Sterilization Act. The following year proceedings were begun to have him sterilized and he resisted on constitutional grounds. The Supreme Court of the United States struck down the statute because, as it was construed under state law, embezzlers could not be subjected to sterilization but those who committed larceny could. Justice Douglas wrote the opinion for the Court and he attacked the statute as an arbitrary classification: "When the law lays an unequal hand on those who have committed intrinsically the same quality of offense and sterilizes one and not the other, it has made as invidious a discrimination as if it had selected a particular race or nationality for oppressive treatment."[11]

The Supreme Court did not decide in Skinner that no sterilization statute could satisfy the requirement of equal protection of the laws. Rather, the decision was based upon the inadequacy of the particular Oklahoma statute. However, the Skinner decision did betoken an attitude of judicial hostility toward sterilization, perhaps as an outgrowth of the use of it in Nazi Germany. In the Skinner decision the Court emphasized the suspect character of compulsory sterilization:

> We are dealing here with legislation which involves one of the basic civil rights of man. Marriage and procreation are fundamental to the very existence and survival of the race. The power to sterilize, if exercised, may have subtle, far-reaching and devastating effects. In evil or reckless hands it can cause races or types which are inimical to the dominant group to wither and disappear. There is no redemption for the individual whom the law touches. Any experiment which the State conducts is to his irreparable injury. He is forever deprived of a basic liberty. We mention these matters . . . merely in emphasis of our view that strict scrutiny of the classification which a State makes in a sterilization law is essential, lest unwittingly or otherwise invidious discriminations are made against groups or types of individuals in violation of the constitutional guaranty of just and equal law.

Apart from whether or not the statute involves an arbitrary classification, sterilization as such is irrelevant as a device to prevent the commission of further crimes by the person sterilized. A burglar would not be drawn away from a second-story career because he has been sterilized. Nor would any other type of criminal be deterred, including the sex offender. Sterilization does not interfere with a man's desire to commit a rape or with a woman's desire to engage in prostitution. Sterilization by castration is, of course, an exception, but castration is not a usual mode of sterilization. Indeed, at least in the case of prostitution, sterilization can encourage crime by removing the fear of pregnancy that can inhibit a woman from engaging in prostitution. It is fair to say, therefore, that the use of sterilization as a penalty for crime cannot be justified as a reasonable measure for the prevention of further crime by the criminal sterilized.

On the other hand, the loss of the reproductive capacity is such a grave consequence that the prospect of sterilization could deter other people from committing crimes. At this point the discussion of equal protection of the laws verges into the area of due process of law. The Fourteenth Amendment provides: "No State shall . . . deprive any person of life, liberty, or property, without due process of law." A similar prohibition in the Fifth Amendment binds the federal government. Due process of law can be either procedural or substantive. Procedural due process would seem to require that no sterilization could be compelled except after a hearing on notice and probably a right of appeal to the courts. The basic requirement of substantive due process of law is that the end to be sought and the means employed must be reasonable. It is debatable whether compulsory sterilization as a punishment for crime does in fact operate to deter others from the commission of any type of crime. Given the constitutional validity of capital punishment, however, it is unlikely that sterilization would be held unconstitutional as a punishment for crime. Whether the prospect of sterilization would deter a person who is contemplating, say, an embezzlement, is conjectural, although we can probably infer that the imposition of such a basic sanction would operate to give at least some persons second thought before committing a crime. In any event, the right to decide the issue would seem to belong to the legislature. The lesser includes the greater. And as long as it can even be plausibly argued that sterilization has some deterrent value, the legitimacy of the death penalty would support the constitutionality of punitive sterilization. It might also be said in its favor that punitive sterilization is an appropriate act of retribution, whereby the community can balance the scales of justice. On the other hand, it can be criticized on the constitutional ground that it inflicts a cruel and unusual punishment. Although it is not technically a maiming at common law, since it does not interfere with the ability to fight, sterilization, arguably, is sufficiently analogous to maiming to be rejected as a reversion to barbarism. On balance, however, it is fair to say that it is within the constitutional power of a legislature to impose sterilization as a penalty for crime, provided that if the statute specifies only certain types of criminals as eligible for the penalty, the classification must be reasonable. But the deficiencies of punitive sterilization are serious and it is hardly prudent, whatever its constitutionality, to impose it in practice.

Nor are the drawbacks of punitive sterilization diminished by recent studies on the effect of chromosomal imbalances.[12] Each cell in a woman's body contains two "X" chromosomes, while each cell in a man's body has one "X" and one "Y." The "Y" chromosome is the genetic material that basically differentiates men from women. About one out of every 2000 men has a chromosomal content of XYY instead of the usual XY. Recent studies, however, have indicated that this genetic abnormality is sixty times as prevalent in men convicted of violent crimes as in the general population. This discovery may open a significant prospect for treatment to reduce criminal tendencies in some offenders. But it does not justify punitive or eugenic sterilization. For it has not yet been proven that this abnormality is hereditarily transmitted in any predictable pattern. Also, even if it were, the XYY abnormality does not automatically impel the possessor to violent or anti-social behavior, as shown by the fact that the vast majority of XYY people are not criminals. The science of genetics can do much to explain and improve the biological conditions of life, but this constructive function cannot be used as an argument for the unfounded use of sterilization for punitive or eugenic purposes.

Punitive sterilization has assumed a renewed importance in light of the increasing efforts being made to sterilize mothers of illegitimate children who are receiving aid under public welfare programs. Dr. Julius Paul of the Walter Reed Army Institute of Research told the 1966 meeting of the American Psychiatric Association that "The numerous unsuccessful efforts at passing punitive sterilization laws in the past decade, aimed largely at mothers of illegitimate children receiving Aid to Dependent Children or other public aid, is evidence enough that American sterilization history, 1907–66, has come full circle. After shifting away from punitive and then strictly eugenic considerations to environmental and social criteria, we are now contemplating using sterilization in a punitive, even vindictive, fashion on some of our nation's most unfortunate and vulnerable people."[13] Sterilization is questionable at best as a punishment for convicted criminals. When directed against welfare recipients, it is vengeful and barbarous. It would fight poverty by eliminating the poor. Instead of curbing welfare bounties, which would impel the easy-living clients to curb their promiscuity out of self-interest, sterilization would encourage promiscuity and would affirm that our aim is not the preservation of the family and the improvement of morals, but rather the avoidance of children. Also, when compulsory sterilization is imposed upon welfare recipients, it has undeniably eugenic overtones. For sterilization is a mode of birth control and, as we have seen in the chapter on contraception, "family planning" is conceived by some as a device to reduce the burgeoning, predominantly Negro populations of the core cities. Implicit in this is the judgment that welfare clients ought not to reproduce themselves. It is eugenic sterilization based on economics rather than genetics.

In its only other ruling on the merits of sterilization (except for Skinner v. Oklahoma), the Supreme Court of the United States in 1927 upheld a Virginia statute providing for the compulsory eugenic sterilization of feeble-minded inmates of certain institutions. Carrie Buck was an eighteen-year-old white girl who was committed to the Virginia State Colony for the Epileptic and Feeble-Minded. She had the mind of a nine-year-old and was the mother of an illegitimate child of defective mentality. Carrie's mother had also been committed to the same colony as a feeble-minded person. The authorities ordered a salpingectomy performed on Carrie pursuant to the Virginia Sterilization Act. Carrie, through her guardian, contended that the sterilization would deprive her of her constitutional rights. The Virginia courts ordered the operation to be performed and Carrie appealed to the Supreme Court of the United States. Justice Oliver Wendell Holmes wrote the opinion for the Court. He rejected the argument that the statute violated the equal protection of the laws because it applied only to feeble-minded persons in certain institutions and not to the feeble-minded who were not institutionalized. He retorted that "the law does all that is needed when it does all that it can, indicates a policy, applies it to all within the lines and seeks to bring within the lines all similarly situated so far and so fast as its means allow. Of course, so far as the operations enable those who otherwise must be kept confined to be returned to the world, and thus open the asylum to others, the equality aimed at will be more nearly reached." Justice Holmes, incidentally, described the equal protection theory as "the last resort of constitutional arguments."[14] Significantly, Justice Holmes compared sterilization to conscription into the military forces: "We have seen more than once that the public welfare may call upon the best citizens for their lives. It would be strange if it could not call upon those who already sap the strength of the State for these lesser sacrifices, often not felt to be such by those concerned, in order to prevent our being swamped with incompetence." He further compared it to vaccination, saying, "The principle that sustains compulsory vaccination is broad enough to cover cutting the Fallopian tubes." Then, in one of his most quoted lines, Holmes decreed, "Three generations of imbeciles are enough."[15] So Carrie Buck was sterilized.

Eugenic sterilization evokes an image of Buchenwald and Auschwitz. But it really is an American export. The first vasectomy was performed in the Indiana State Reformatory in 1889. The first compulsory sterilization statute was enacted in that state in 1907. Twenty-seven states now have laws requiring sterilization in certain cases. Five of these provide for voluntary as well as compulsory sterilization. Two other states have purely voluntary laws. In all twenty-nine states, the acts apply to the feeble-minded, to the insane in twenty-six, to the epileptic in about half, to the habitual criminal in about a third, and to the moral degenerate and sex pervert in about one fifth.[16] More than 65,000 persons have been sterilized under these statutes, most of them females. An undetermined number have been sterilized privately for therapeutic or contraceptive reasons.

Eugenic sterilization laws grew out of the eugenic movement that was initiated in the late nineteenth century by Sir Francis Galton, a relative and follower of Charles Darwin. The basic assumption of the movement was that the human stock could be improved by restricting the right or capacity of defective persons to breed. The notion was reinforced by Gregor Mendel's announcement of his "unit particle" rule in 1900. Three of Mendel's theories are relevant to our problem. Mendel's first law, of dominance, held that when two pure-bred organisms with contrasting characters, or traits, are mated the offspring will show only one of the characters, the dominant one. The trait that does not appear in these first-generation offspring is termed recessive. His second law postulated that characters are transmitted to the offspring without being changed or lost. Mendel's third law held that a hidden recessive character may reappear as a dominant trait in a later generation of offspring. Mendel's theories were based upon his studies of plants, but their implications for human breeding are obvious. However, there are weaknesses in the uncritical application of these theories in sterilization laws. One is that mental or other defects may be recessive. Though not apparent in one generation they may reappear in a later generation. Therefore, if sterilization is ever to eradicate the transmission of defects, it will have to be applied to recessive carriers of defective characters as well as to persons whom we see to be actually defective. But carriers far outnumber defectives and they cannot be identified with precision. It would be wholly impractical as well as oppressive to extend compulsory sterilization so far.

Regardless of the administrative problems, scientists today strongly doubt that mental or physical defects are transmissible simply by heredity. One of the leading studies supporting the sterilization movement was published in 1912 by Henry Goddard, who concluded that mental defects were transmitted from generation to generation.[17] The assumptions of this study have been challenged in more recent times. One critic attacked the completeness of the data upon which Goddard based his conclusions:

> . . . the criteria which Goddard used to diagnose mental deficiency are very vaguely stated and the field data only sketchily presented . . . the amount of error involved in the interpretation of a field worker's observations, based sometimes on secondary and tertiary sources, must be considerable. Goddard's diagnostic labels have an unknown degree of reliability and validity which imposes serious limitations on his conclusions.[18]

Dr. Walter E. Fernald, a leading advocate of sterilization, himself repudiated his views in an essay published after his death. He denied the easy assumption that defects are hereditary and called instead for sympathetic treatment of defectives:

> For nearly two decades the whole tendency of public opinion and of legislative action was to ignore the rights and privileges of the individual defective and to treat him harshly and almost punitively. He was looked upon as an Ishmaelite, as an invariably useless, dangerous person, who should be ostracized, sterilized and segregated for his natural life at public expense. . . . But within a few years many things have happened to make us believe that we have been far too sweeping in some of our generalizations and deductions concerning the feeble-minded. . . . Nearly every plan for dealing with the feeble-minded implies that every case is of the hereditary group but certain common types of defect are always non-hereditary, such as the mongolian idiot, cases of focal brain lesion with resulting spastic paralysis and mental defect, cases caused by injury to the brain at birth or during infancy, acute inflammation of the brain or membranes, syphilis, cretinism, etc. . . . the proverbial badness of the "Kallikak" or "Jukes" types of defective is perhaps due to his surroundings as much as to his heredity. . . . We have seen that

our knowledge of feeble-mindedness is gradually increasing as the result of scientific study and observation in many fields: medical, legal, and eugenic. We now know that feeble-mindedness is not an entity, to be dealt with in a routine way, but is an infinitely complex problem.[19]

The basic premise of the eugenic sterilization movement has yielded to scientific proof. As one observer put it in 1955:

The program grew out of a belief that heredity is responsible for a large amount of crime, poverty, mental deficiency, illness, and social depravity. This belief, or opinion, was not justified by the facts and scientific evidence at hand and was not advocated by geneticists. . . .[20]

Compulsory sterilization for eugenic purposes is today little more than an exercise in witchcraft. It is also inhuman, stupid, and wasteful. It would have deprived the world of such figures as Hans Christian Andersen, Balzac, Beethoven, Byron, Diderot, Frederick the Great, Goethe, Michelangelo, Newton, Poe, Strindberg, Swift, and Tolstoy—all of whose ancestry included mental illness or epilepsy sufficient to warrant sterilization of the ancestor under our statutes.[21]

On the other hand, sterilization is effective if one desires to exterminate an easily definable race. In Nazi Germany sterilization of Jews was carried out on a large scale and extensive experiments were conducted, without notable success, to develop easier and cheaper ways to sterilize with drugs and X rays. Heinrich Himmler's objective was "not only to defeat the enemy but to exterminate him. The capacity for work of the sterilized persons could be exploited by Germany, while the danger of propagation would be eliminated. As this mass sterilization was part of Himmler's racial theory, particular time and care were devoted to these sterilization experiments. . . . It was further desired that a procedure be found which would result in sterilization that was not immediately noticeable."[22]

Sterilization today is mainly important as a contraceptive method. In India a bill was nearly enacted in 1967 that would have required the sterilization of all fathers after the birth of their third child.[23] The Indian program is still voluntary, although cash incentives are paid to men to induce them to submit to vasectomy. In the United States, Great Britain, and elsewhere, contraceptive sterilization is a big and growing business. National surveys indicate that birth control by voluntary sterilization is acceptable to a majority of the people in the United States. A Gallup Poll has shown that 64% of the American people approve of voluntary sterilization as a birth control method.[24] Professor Judson Landis of the Institute of Human Development in Berkeley, California, estimates that "About two million men and women in the United States have reportedly chosen sterilization as a contraceptive measure."[25] The Association for Voluntary Sterilization, Inc., claims to have a nationwide list of 1600 cooperating physicians and asserts that more than 100,000 Americans each year, 60% of them women, choose voluntary sterilization as a method of family planning.[26] A new organization, the International Association for Voluntary Sterilization, was formed in December 1967 "to conduct education on voluntary sterilization on a world level." Its honorary chairman is Dr. Brock Chisholm, first director general of the World Health Organization. The Simon Population Trust recently reported that at least 10,000 British married couples have sought sterilization there in the past two years. In almost every case, the report said, it is the husband who undergoes the operation.[27] Contraceptive sterilization is legal in England and in the United States. In Connecticut and Utah it is a crime to perform a sterilization, except pursuant to an existing compulsory eugenic sterilization statute or for "medical necessity."[28] These statutes, however, are probably insufficient to prevent contraceptive sterilization, owing to their use of the elastic term "medical necessity."

Only the Catholic Church, among religious bodies, is officially opposed to direct sterilization for eugenic or contraceptive purposes. The Church regards it as an illicit mutilation, whether voluntary or involuntary. In the words of Pope Pius XI:

> Public magistrates have no direct power over the bodies of their subjects; therefore, where no crime has taken place and there is no cause present for grave punishment, they can never directly harm or tamper with the integrity of the body, either for the reasons of eugenics or for any other reason. . . .
>
> Furthermore . . . private individuals have no other power over the members of their bodies than that which pertains to their natural ends; and they are not free to destroy or mutilate their members, or in any other way render themselves unfit for their natural functions, except when no other provision can be made for the good of the whole body. . . ."[29]

Pope Paul reiterated this condemnation in his 1968 encyclical, *Humanae Vitae*. The Anglican Lambeth Conference of 1958 opposed compulsory eugenic sterilization as "unacceptable to the Christian conscience."[30] Other religious leaders are more flexible. For instance, Dr. Joseph Fletcher says, "It is impossible to see how the principle of social justice . . . can be satisfied if the community may not defend itself, and is forced to permit the continued procreation of feeble-minded or hereditarily diseased children."[31] Non-Catholic theologians are more frequently inclined to favor voluntary than compulsory sterilization. The Church of England, for example, has indicated a limited approval for voluntary sterilization in particularly compelling cases.[32] Methodist Bishop John Wesley Lord of Washington, D.C., has strongly endorsed the practice in these words:

> I personally believe that voluntary sterilization, when determined as necessary by competent authorities, and if practiced in Christian conscience, fulfills rather than violates the will of God. Indications for or against sterilization should, I believe, include socio-economic as well as moral factors.[33]

As a contraceptive technique, sterilization is open to all the objections that are relevant as a matter of principle to contraception by other means. But sterilization is essentially different because it involves a change of status. It is more than a pill or device that does not permanently destroy the future capacity to reproduce. Sterilization by surgical means is, in practical terms, irrevocable. If we are to achieve a coherent program to protect the integrity of the family and to promote respect for life, it would seem reasonable to restrict the performance of merely contraceptive sterilizations.

It would be easy to say that contraceptive sterilization should be prohibited by law just as the law should restrict the sale and distribution of contraceptives, at least to minors. However, it would be unwise to impose such a prohibition. Any regulation in this area must be consistent with the right to privacy and the legitimate requirements of medical practice. For example, suppose a wife cannot endure another pregnancy without grave danger to her life. If she voluntarily obtains a salpingectomy, the operation is directly contraceptive and indirectly therapeutic. Her operation is not forbidden by the law in the United States today. Nor should it be. There is, arguably, reasonable medical necessity for the operation in her case.

For the law to forbid the operation would involve an undue intrusion into the professional judgment of the doctor as well as into the patient's privacy. Unlike abortion, there is no third person in the womb to be considered here. Rather, it would seem preferable to hedge such operations about with procedural safeguards to ensure that they are not employed for merely contraceptive reasons. The filing of adequate reports could be required and the enforcement of the sanction could safely be entrusted to the licensing agencies and the medical profession. On the other hand, the criminal law should punish the performance of merely contraceptive sterilizations. Such a law would have to be carefully drawn to exclude cases in which a reasonable medical necessity is shown. Perhaps the filing of a required postoperative report with a licensing agency should be a complete defense to a criminal prosecution. The sanction for filing a fraudulent report to cover the performance of an illicit sterilization could be limited to professional and licensing penalties. As a practical matter, therefore, the criminal penalties could be reserved for those doctors who operate sterilization mills and perform purely contraceptive operations with a willful criminal intent.

For the law to refrain from punishing every contraceptive sterilization as a crime would not connote approval of the practice. On the contrary, the limited sanction should be adopted only because a total prohibition would unduly impinge upon basic personal rights and medical practice. The primary goal should be the elimination of sterilization as a contraceptive or eugenic device. The law can and should discourage its use for that purpose.

It is about time, too, for the law to advance from the Dark Ages and outlaw eugenic sterilization. The laws requiring such sterilization should be repealed and the operation for eugenic purposes should be forbidden, even where voluntarily undergone. Punitive sterilization laws should also be repealed because they are largely irrelevant to the prevention of crime and because their continuance could serve as a cloak for eugenic sterilization of convicted criminals.

A reversal of the current law and a restriction of sterilization would not be an unduly severe remedy. The popularity of sterilization stems from the prevalent abdication of personal accountability for one's own acts. Our generation, too, is unwilling to take responsibility for others, whether their neighbors or the unborn. As long as sterilization is compulsorily imposed upon "defectives" or freely available for contraceptive purposes, it will feed the growth of irresponsibility. In other words, it is inconceivable that we can ever restore personal responsibility as long as we condone an act so symbolic of the shirking of obligation in an era saturated with self-indulgence. Sterilization also can readily be used as a tool of oppression. It must be curtailed, even when it is voluntary, or else we shall have to contend with an expansion of it as a compulsory weapon in the arsenal of the caretaker state.

Contraception and sterilization involve a defiance of nature. And their prevalence is symptomatic of the irresponsibility with which we are basically concerned. But our treatment of these efforts to liberate the sexual act from its consequences would be incomplete without some consideration of another and even more striking perversion of the procreational faculty. Homosexuality could not be seriously contending for respectability, as it is, if our society had not forgotten some of the basic truths of life, love, and marriage. Instead, particularly in some intellectual quarters, we are increasingly unable to formulate a rational condemnation of homosexuality. This is partly because we have forgotten that rights and privileges cannot rightly be enjoyed in willful isolation from their attendant responsibilities. The homosexual issue is not as practically important as some others we have discussed. But it is symbolic and it does provide a measure of our decline. For this reason we turn to it as our final topic.

9

HOMOSEXUALITY

Teen culture back in my Illinois home town during World War II had a simple way of dealing with homosexuals. Our high-school football heroes beat them up. Just for the hell of it. Horsing around outside a Nash show-room recommissioned as the Idle Hour, one of our beefy tackles would wait to be picked up by a G.I. He would lead his victim down the alley toward the Knights of Pythias park. Then, wham! The rest of the squad would lay the poor soldier out, perhaps relieve him of his watch, hop into a Model A and head for the B-Z-B. Mexican wimpies and lots of laughs for everyone. It got so bad Scott Field had to station M.P.'s outside the tavern like door-men.[1]

The homosexual has never been Saturday's hero in America or anywhere else. At least so far. The term "homosexual" is derived from the Greek *homo*, which means "the same as." Homosexuality, therefore, is a sexual propensity for persons of one's own sex, whether male or female. The terms "lesbian" and "sapphic" refer to sexual relations between women. The Greek poetess Sappho was homosexual and she lived on the island of Lesbos.

The Kinsey Report estimated that 4% of adult white males in America are exclusively and permanently homosexual after they reach adolescence and that 37% have had some actual homosexual experience at some time in their lives.[2] Other estimates range much higher than 4%, as seen in one book with the descriptive title, *The Sixth Man.*[3]

With the exception of Illinois, which repealed in 1961 its prohibition against private homosexual acts between adults, all the American states punish such acts as crimes. The prohibited acts are variously defined and the penalties range from a three-month maximum in New York to a possible life imprisonment in Nevada.[4] The United States is one of a minority of nations, including the Soviet Union and West Germany, that punish such homosexual acts.

In 1967, Great Britain repealed its prohibitions against sexual acts committed in private between consenting adults. This action followed the recommendations of the Wolfenden Committee, which submitted its report to Parliament in 1957. The Wolfenden Committee emphasized the distinction between "homosexual offenses," which are punished by the law, and "homosexuality," which is "a sexual propensity for persons of one's own sex." Homosexuality is a personal status or condition and cannot properly be punished by the criminal law.[5] Nor is homosexuality an all-or-nothing condition. "All gradations can exist from apparently exclusive homosexuality without any conscious capacity for arousal by heterosexual stimuli to apparently exclusive heterosexuality, though in the latter case there may be transient and minor homosexual inclinations, for instance in adolescence."[6] Moreover, "It must not be thought the existence of the homosexual propensity necessarily leads to homosexual behavior of an overtly sexual kind."[7]

The Wolfenden Report was based on the notion that:

Unless a deliberate attempt is to be made by society, acting through the agency of the law, to equate the sphere of crime with that of sin, there must remain a realm of private morality and immorality which is, in brief and crude terms, not the law's business.[8]

Similarly, the American Law Institute in 1955 urged the relaxation of laws against homosexual acts, on the ground that:

No harm to the secular interests of the community is involved in atypical sexual practice in private between consenting adult partners. This area of private morals is the distinctive concern of spiritual authorities.[9]

Illinois followed the American Law Institute recommendation in repealing its prohibition in 1961.

Homosexuality is a big business in the United States today. There are homosexual clubs with high initiation fees. There are "gay bars," where members of the breed congregate, in every major city from coast to coast. The traveling homosexual can even buy a directory of these places so that he need never lack companionship. Homosexual pornography occupies an increasingly major share of the market in obscene materials. Columbia University recently chartered the Student Homophile League, the first homosexual organization to be officially recognized by a university in the United States.[10] It is in New York City "that the 'third sex' is establishing a national capital." According to one New York County prosecutor, "the tendency in recent years here has been to be less severe in dealing with homosexuals." Job opportunities are better for homosexuals in New York City and, as one member of the Mattachine Society put it, "There is a social maturity in New York City toward homosexuals. Since Lindsay came into office we've made important breakthroughs in many fields. This increasingly tolerant atmosphere is one reason more homosexuals are coming to New York."[11]

The homosexual magazine, *One*, claims a national circulation of 5000. There are many similar publications on a smaller scale. The North American Homophile Conference has a membership of around 6000. Drew Shafer, a thirty-one-year-old homosexual who is an officer of the Conference, says that the homosexual longs to be free to hold a job, to advance in the professions, to serve in the armed forces, to advocate the cause of homosexuality, and to practice it without fear of reprisal. He strongly advocates that homosexual marriages be legalized: "One thing the homosexual doesn't want is to grow old alone."[12] Others emphasize legal marriage as the goal because it would offer economic advantages through the filing of joint income tax returns and joint ownership of property. Some have even suggested that homosexual couples be permitted to adopt children.[13] The average homosexual marriage, incidentally, lasts no more than three or four years.

It would be unfair to dismiss these ideas out of hand as bizarre and ludicrous without seriously trying to understand the dimensions of the human problem involved. The committed homosexual is a person suspended between two worlds. His predicament is pathetic and it properly deserves compassion rather than ridicule. However, sympathy for those ensnared ought not to obscure the fact that they are advancing an idea that threatens, in principle, the family structure and our heritage of Judaeo-Christian morality. They seek to have homosexual acts considered natural and treated on a par with the heterosexual. In this, not surprisingly, they have support from liberal clergymen. The Rev. Edward Schillebeeckx, an avant-garde Jesuit of the Dutch Catholic Church, recently criticized the controversial Dutch catechism because it merely notes that it is "not the fault of the individual if he or she is not attracted to the other sex."

This does not go far enough to suit Father Schillebeeckx. "The problem is that this makes no moral judgment. Many theologians now think we should say that, in some situations for some men, homosexuality is a moral good because it is the only manner in which they can experience sexuality."[14]

In November 1967 ninety Episcopalian priests met in New York City as part of Project H, a symposium on homosexuality. Most participants appeared to agree with the Rev. Walter D. Dennis, canon of the Cathedral of St. John the Divine, that "A homosexual relationship between two adults should be judged by the same criteria as a heterosexual marriage—that is, whether it is intended to foster a permanent relationship of love."[15] One member of the minority warned against "the lessening of moral restraints in society." Another declared that homosexual acts "must always be regarded as perversions because they are not part of the natural process of rearing children. The reason for breaking down one ethical standard may affect others, like the stability of marriage," he warned. Traditional Catholic and Protestant thinking as well as Mosaic and Talmudic law regard homosexual acts as abominable and sinful.

Those who would remove the prohibition against private homosexual acts between consenting adults frequently rely on John Stuart Mill, who wrote, in his essay, "On Liberty":

> The object of this Essay is to assert one simple principle. . . . That principle is, that the sole end for which mankind are warranted, individually or collectively in interfering with the liberty of action of any of their number, is self-protection. That the only purpose for which power can be rightfully exercised over any member of a civilized community, against his will, is to prevent harm to others. His own good, either physical or moral, is not a sufficient warrant. He cannot rightfully be compelled to do or forbear because it will be better for him to do so, because it will make him happier, because in the opinions of others, to do so would be wise or even right. . . . The only part of the conduct of any one, for which he is amenable to society, is that which concerns others.[16]

The theory is that adults who voluntarily commit homosexual acts in private do no harm to other people. If they hurt anyone by their conduct, it is only themselves and their mutual consent should operate to bar a criminal penalty for that. Some advocates of this position would depart from Mill's rigorous doctrine so as to allow the law to make it a crime to inflict *physical* harm on another even if he consents.[17] But supporters of the Wolfenden thesis reject laws against private homosexual acts because, in their opinion, they are designed to prevent merely *moral* harm to the consenting adult. However, this position is not well taken.

Committee member James Adair directly challenged the basic premise of *The Wolfenden Report*, that private activity should not be made criminal unless it causes direct harm to other individuals, and claimed correctly that the Committee had itself violated the premise by approving a different rule for minors:

> The fact that activities inherently hurtful to community life are carried out clandestinely and in privacy does not adequately justify the removal of such conduct from the criminal code. It is indisputable that many acts committed in private may be contrary to the public good and as such fall under the criminal law. In my view, homosexual acts are of this class, and the mere fact that the discrimination made by the majority of the Committee by which freedom from control is not recommended for persons between eighteen and twenty-one years of age is a definite recognition of this principle. . . .[18]

The rigid limitation that the criminal law can prohibit an act only if it causes harm to other persons is an oversimplification. As generally stated by those who would soften the laws against homosexuality, the proposition seems to require a fairly direct connection between the defendant's conduct and the injury or damage suffered by some identifiable, non-consenting person who is measurably harmed. However, this is not the only type of harm that the criminal law can seek to prevent. There is a more basic and more pervasive harm that can be done to society and ultimately but necessarily to each person, through the weakening of the family structure and the erosion of those principled restraints on behavior that we sometimes describe as decencies but that are in fact necessities. When the law prohibits homosexual acts, wherever and by whomever committed, it does not act arbitrarily or in enforcement of an esoteric moral code that happens to be now prevailing but that has no further claim to recognition than the tenets of Timothy Leary's League for Spiritual Discovery. The laws against homosexuality are part of an integrated structure designed to preserve the basic unit, the family, which in turn depends on the cultivation of a continuing regard for life and the processes by which it is created. And this is reasonable.

The law cannot legitimately prohibit men from shaking hands or telling jokes together, whether in public or in private, unless an actual breach of the peace or some other independent crime is committed. But the act of generation has a profound significance beyond the shaking of hands or the telling of jokes. It is the act upon which the very preservation of the species depends. When that act is perverted from its purpose, the law can hardly look the other way with indifference.

It is important, though, to remember that what is involved here is action, not speech. Nor is it the solitary action of self-abuse, which clearly should be protected by the right of privacy against government intrusion. Nor is it an unnatural act committed in the privacy of marriage, where the government should not interfere just as it should not punish the use of contraceptives by married persons. Rather, what we have here is an act involving two adults, both of the same sex, who perform a perverted travesty of marital relations. Their act is secret, but to regard it with indifference is to condone it. A relaxation of the law predictably would cause more young men and perhaps women to experiment with homosexual acts. The harm to persons who so indulge is more than merely moral. It is social and perhaps economic. If harm to others is the indispensable requirement for enforcement of the criminal law, the harm to potential initiates into the deviate fraternity should suffice. But even if it were shown that relaxation of the law would not induce a single person to indulge in homosexual acts, there would still be sufficient reason to continue the prohibition. For there is a generalized harm to the family, to society, and to its members, from an implicit legitimation of conduct so basically at war with the endurance of the family.

Also, for the protection of the family, the law can legitimately foster virtue to a limited extent by forbidding vice. As Sir Patrick Devlin said, "It is wrong to talk of private morality or of the law not being concerned with immorality as such or to try to set rigid bounds to the part which the law may play in the suppression of vice."[19]

It is important that the Wolfenden Committee inquired whether homosexuality is a disease. As the Committee noted, "There are two important practical consequences which are often thought to follow from regarding homosexuality as an illness. The first is that those in whom the condition exists are sick persons and should therefore be regarded as medical problems and consequently as primarily a medical responsibility. The second is that sickness implies irresponsibility, or at least diminished responsibility."[20] The Committee concluded, "We feel bound to say that the evidence put before us has not established to our satisfaction the proposition that homosexuality is a disease."[21] Furthermore, "Even if it could be established that homosexuality were a disease, it is clear that many individuals, however their state is reached, present social rather than medical problems and must be dealt with by social, including penological, methods."[22]

The Wolfenden Committee denied that homosexual acts were "compulsive" or inherently irresistible, and concluded instead that "there seems to be no good reason to suppose that at least in the majority of cases homosexual acts are any more or less resistible than heterosexual acts, and other evidence would be required to sustain such a view in any individual case. Even if immunity from penal sanctions on such grounds were claimed or granted, nevertheless preventive measures would have to be taken for the sake of society at large, in much the same way as it is necessary to withhold a driving license from a person who is subject to epileptic fits."[23] Incidentally, there is evidence that homosexuality is not congenital or inherited but rather is acquired in some way. As one study concluded:

> Homosexuality is acquired; it is not congenital nor inherited. It is the behavior symptom of a deep-seated and unresolved neurosis. Homosexuals, themselves, prefer to believe they were born that way. They delude themselves into thinking that their homosexuality is caused by a congenital constitutional defect or some hormone imbalance. Dr. Clifford Allen stated quite emphatically that sexual inversion is not a congenital anomaly: "Much has been said of the congenital and endocrine types of homosexuality but there is not the slightest vestige of evidence that this condition is congenital or endocrine."[24]

There is reason to believe, also, that homosexuals are afflicted with a compulsive urge to proselytize and recruit new members to the fraternity or sorority as the case may be. If this is so, relaxation of the existing prohibitions could result in a substantial increase of homosexual activity through recruitment pursued by means short of the offensive public solicitation that is still forbidden in England

and Illinois. This proselytizing tendency could assume particular importance in the case of the homosexual teacher. As Dr. Morton Friedman of the New Jersey College of Medicine put it:

> His tolerance for frustration, for delay of gratification, is much less than that of the average heterosexual, and this frequently leads to a compulsive quality in his sexual drive which is seldom seen in adult heterosexuals. Because of this, contrary to the anonymous opinion expressed in letters recently, the homosexual teacher is much more likely to become involved with his male students than the heterosexual teacher is with female students. The same likelihood has also been noted with female homosexual teachers.[25]

It would be a mistake, however, to treat homosexual behavior as a problem of purely criminal dimensions. There is much that can be done by medicine and psychiatry, to say nothing of religion, in this area. Unfortunately the repeal of the penalties for private homosexual activity would remove one of the main incentives impelling homosexuals to obtain professional help for their condition. The proper aim of the law should be to help these pathetic people. And sometimes help can best be provided in the form of an *in terrorem* motive to reform.

The main reason, however, for punishing private homosexual acts is that punishment would serve to reinforce the family as the basic unit of society. The growth of homosexuality is at once a result of the prevalent family breakdown and a cause of a further acceleration of that breakdown. The Wolfenden Committee noted that "in the general loosening of former moral standards, it would not be surprising to find that leniency toward sexual irregularities in general included also an increased tolerance of homosexual behavior and that greater tolerance had encouraged the practice."[26] Also, "it is likely that the emotional insecurity, community instability and weakening of the family, inherent in the social changes of our civilization, have been factors contributing to an increase in homosexual behavior."[27]

Interestingly, the Wolfenden Committee agreed that homosexuality has a damaging effect on family life. Curiously, however, the Committee argued that female homosexuality has a damaging effect equal to that of the male variety. Since the English law does not punish lesbian behavior, the Committee felt it should not punish homosexual acts by males. The idea seemed to be that both should be punished or neither and that, since no one seriously was suggesting that lesbian acts should now be made a crime, therefore male homosexual acts should no longer be criminal.

It is worth while to quote the Committee on the effect of homosexual acts in destroying the family:

The second contention, that homosexual behavior between males has a damaging effect on family life, may well be. Indeed, we have had evidence that it often is; cases in which homosexual behavior on the part of the husband has broken up a marriage are by no means rare, and there are also cases in which a man in whom the homosexual component is relatively weak nevertheless derives such satisfaction from homosexual outlets that he does not enter upon a marriage which might have been successfully and happily consummated. . . . We have had no reasons shown to us which would lead us to believe that homosexual behavior between males inflicts any greater damage on family life than adultery, fornication or lesbian behavior. These practices are all reprehensible from the point of view of harm to the family, but it is difficult to see why on this ground male homosexual behavior alone among them should be a criminal offense. This argument is not to be taken as saying that society should condone or approve male homosexual behavior. But where adultery, fornication and lesbian behavior are not criminal offenses there seems to us to be no valid ground, on the basis of damage to the family, for so regarding homosexual behavior between men.[28]

The Committee is sound in its premise that adultery, fornication, lesbian behavior, and homosexual acts should be treated equally as far as criminal punishment is concerned. But rather than conclude that none of them should be punished, the Committee would have been more in accord with its concern for the family if it had urged instead that they all be punished so far as it is practical to do so without an undue invasion of privacy.

Committee member James Adair emphasized in his dissent the bad effect the relaxation would have "on the whole moral fabric of social life."[29] He warned:

The influence of example in forming the views and developing the characters of young people can scarcely be overestimated. The presence in a district of, for example, adult male lovers living openly and notoriously under the approval of the law is bound to have a regrettable and pernicious effect on the young people of the community. No one interested in the moral, physical or spiritual welfare of public life wishes to see homosexuality extending in its scope, but rather reduced in extent, or at least kept effectively in check.[30]

Mr. Adair argued that "the current relaxed attitude toward moral conduct and relationships, so prevalent everywhere, makes the present an inopportune time for loosening bonds and removing restrictions. . . ."[31] He deplored the sentimentalism that focuses on the person who is by nature homosexual.

> These considerations [he argued] have been allowed to obscure the other type who, in the absence of any innate tendency, whether from monetary or other reasons, takes up this type of behavior, and have tended, too, to obscure the interests of the public in general and the decent self-disciplined citizen in particular.[32]

Those who would relax the homosexual laws emphasize that they would retain the prohibitions against such things as indecent assaults and public solicitation, which do offend public sensibilities and invade the rights of unwilling victims. They maintain, too, that the prohibition against consensual homosexual acts in private is practically unenforceable without an outrageous invasion of privacy. In Griswold v. Connecticut[33] in 1965, the Supreme Court upset the Connecticut ban on the use of contraceptives because its enforcement would involve an undue intrusion into the marital relationship. Justice William O. Douglas, for the majority of the Court, wrote, "Would we allow the police to search the sacred precincts of marital bedrooms for telltale signs of the use of contraceptives? The very idea is repulsive to the notions of privacy surrounding the marriage relationship."[34] A similar invasion might be seen in the enforcement of a homosexual statute against consenting adults acting in private, except that the marital relation is not involved. The right of privacy ought to prevent completely any official intrusion into the exercise of marital rights. However, homosexual relations cannot be accorded a similar privacy without making a travesty of society's endorsement of marriage. Much as the learned clergy might pretend to the contrary, it is not a matter of indifference whether boys marry girls or other boys.

One insistent argument in favor of relaxation is that the present law fosters blackmail of those in public life who secretly engage in homosexual acts. There have been several cases in recent years in which prominent men have fallen victim to blackmailers on this account. One nationwide ring extorted money from at least two deans of Eastern universities, prominent theatrical personalities, and officers of the armed forces. Two members of the gang, which operated for nearly ten years, even walked into the Pentagon, posing as New York City detectives, and walked out with a high-ranking military officer. They shook the officer down for several thousand dollars. He later committed suicide the night before he was to testify before a New York County grand jury.[35] The homosexual in government employment is an obvious security risk, particularly if he happens to be in a position to reveal secret information under threat of exposure by agents of a foreign power. But it should be remembered that the social stigma would remain even if we moderated the criminal sanctions. Prominent persons who commit homosexual acts would still fear exposure to public condemnation, perhaps even more than they now fear a fine or brief imprisonment. Therefore, although the terror of exposure would be lessened, since it would mean disgrace but not a criminal conviction, relaxation would not materially alleviate the blackmail problem. For the fear of public obloquy would still be strong enough to induce a capitulation to the blackmailer's demand. Nor can it be expected that modification of the criminal sanction would change public opinion so that homosexual acts would no longer be regarded as detestable.

Homosexuality will always be generally regarded as a repulsive deviation. It is so contrary to nature and would be so obviously destructive of the social order if it were generally practiced that it is sheer illusion to think that a mere relaxation of the penal law would make it right and acceptable. However, the proposed change would have one effect. While it would not change the attitude of the unafflicted public, it would encourage susceptible persons to cross from the status of homosexuality to the active practice of homosexual acts. A relaxation of the law would amount to official approval of homosexual acts. However much this might be sincerely denied as the purpose of the change, it would be its effect. The issue is not whether, in the first instance, the homosexual acts in question should have been punished by the criminal law. If it were, then a decision to exclude them from the penal law and to leave them to the sanction of opinion and religion would not necessarily connote approval of those acts. But to remove a sanction after it has been in effect for centuries is not the same as to decide, as a matter of first impression, not to put it in at all. The fact is that the criminal law does punish private homosexual acts between consenting adults. That law cannot be changed without implying approval, or at least a benign tolerance, for those acts. Especially is this true when the change is sought by the homosexuals themselves, who have organized to secure that very approval. Moreover, this difficulty could not be avoided by a mere declaration in the law that homosexual acts are against public policy or even that they are a grave social wrong. Unless the penalty remains, the implication of approval is inescapable. Relaxation of the law would also deprive young men beginning their careers of an objective reason to resist the advances of superiors who would have them commit homosexual acts as the price of preferment. This would appear to be a particular problem in the arts and, to a lesser extent perhaps, in business and the professions.

This book is an appeal for a renewed reverence for life. Legalization of homosexual acts, in any manner and to any degree, can only have the opposite effect. For respect for life entails a regard for all its aspects, including its source. One evil effect of contraception is that it willfully separates the generative from the pleasurable. The act in which life is begun is deliberately turned aside, by artificial means, from any possibility of achieving this end. The possible generation of life is thus regarded as a nuisance and responsibility is evaded. If this is true of contraception, how much more is it true of homosexuality. What a parody of civilized society it would be were it a matter of legal indifference whether sexual intercourse occurred between man and woman or between two of the same sex. It has been seriously proposed by the homosexual groups that homosexual marriages be legitimized and raised to a parity with heterosexual unions. In fact the proposed elimination of the penalty on private homosexual acts between consenting adults would permit such "marriages" to flourish on a de facto basis, avowedly and undisturbed.

Perhaps encouraged by the Supreme Court's absolutist interpretations of freedom of speech, the trend in some quarters is to consider all ideas as having an equal claim to public expression whether the idea be the theory of evolutionary socialism or the proper technique for making napalm bombs to throw at the police. It is but a short step from the assumption that all ideas have an equal right to be heard to the relativist conclusion that competing ideas have equal validity simply because they are competing for approval.

According to this erroneous theory, whichever idea gains popular approval is therefore true. As Justice Oliver Wendell Holmes once wrote, "the best test of truth is the power of the thought to get itself accepted in the market."[36] The proponents of homosexual equality have the right to change the law so as to achieve that equality. But we ought to have no illusions about the implications of adopting their proposals. We can adopt them only if we implicitly but inescapably acknowledge that their idea is as true as the concept of the heterosexual family. But to acknowledge that would be to undermine that family and to file a confession of civic and intellectual bankruptcy.

The drive to relax the homosexual laws reflects an unwillingness to make value judgments as to the rightness or wrongness of conduct. A similar trend is seen in the other areas treated in this book. Our treatment of homosexuals in the past has been primitive and even cruel. But wrong as that attitude was, the proposed suspension of judgment is worse. Instead of condemning the vice and helping the individual homosexual, too many people today allow their sympathy for the deviate to lead them to approve his vice. Unconsciously, in fact, they adopt a perverted value system in their effort to flee from the necessity of making value judgments. As one doctor put it:

> The backlash of society's persecution of homosexuals is being expressed today by our being too ready to declare all values as being equal in worth to humanity, even in the instance in which one set of values represents the infantile needs of individuals and is therefore harmful to a mature society. Much of the display of narcissism and the tendency toward irresponsible hedonism in contemporary society is rooted in and sustained by the homosexual "value system."[37]

A coherent as well as free society requires a frank and unashamed promotion of basic morality in so far as that promotion is consistent with liberty. In no area is this more important than in matters that concern the family.

While it is important to retain and strengthen the criminal prohibitions against homosexual acts, we can and should improve the method of dealing with those acts. It would be worth while for the courts, in appropriate cases, to forgo confinement of homosexual first offenders. Compulsory medical or psychiatric treatment, as deemed best by the court in a secret and unpublicized hearing, could steer some of those first offenders away from a further career of deviate behavior.[38] The treatment could be on an outpatient basis or for a specific and fairly brief term in an institution, as determined by the court. After the first offense, the courts should retain the power to order treatment in lieu of imprisonment, where it would be in the best interests of society and the defendant to do so. However, there will undoubtedly be cases where both first and repeated offenders should be fined or imprisoned or both. The courts should not hesitate to impose these penalties in appropriate cases. It is true that putting a homosexual in prison is "a little like throwing brer rabbit into a brierpatch."[39] But imprisonment can serve a limited though effective purpose here. The prospect of extended jail terms and substantial fines for future offenses would be a salutary deterrent, multiplying the reformative potential of any treatment administered for prior offenses. In short, our policy should aim toward the reduction of homosexual activity rather than its toleration. This end is to be sought, not out of hostility toward those afflicted with deviant tendencies, and not as a blind and emotional reaction. Rather, the task is to strengthen the family, to promote responsibility, and to instill respect for life.

10

THE FUTURE

In April 1968 several hundred Columbia students seized five campus buildings for a week, holding a dean captive in the process. Ostensibly they protested the university's construction of a gymnasium in Morningside Park. But they also dramatized the two accelerating tendencies that are the concern of this book. One is a self-centered rejection of responsibility for others: the insurrectionists disregarded the rights of the majority of Columbia students, who wanted to pursue their studies in order and peace. The other tendency is the flight from accountability for one's own acts: here, too, the revolting students excelled when they demanded that the school grant them total amnesty.

The popular response to the affair was puzzlement and shock. Columbia University bears such an aura of prestige and solidity that a revolution within its walls is incongruous and alarming. People wondered what was the reason for this and what will be next.

The Columbia revolt was part of a world-wide pattern of student revolution, stretching from Bogota to Paris to Tokyo. The nature of that revolution and its function in neutralizing the defenses of the free nations against Communism require a separate study and they are beyond the scope of this book. Rather, we should note here only the role that is played by the erosion of responsibility in smoothing the road toward revolution. The disintegration of personal responsibility, and its accompanying rejection of authority, are evident at all levels of society. The revolts at Columbia and other campuses are emblematic of this deeper malady.

Unless we reverse the tendency to abdicate one's responsibility for others and to deny liability for one's own voluntary acts, we can have little hope of improving our situation. More basically, we need an increased awareness of our responsibility to God, Who obliges us to think not only of ourselves but of others as well and Who, in settling our stewardship, will hold us accountable for our own acts.

Fortunately or unfortunately, as the case may be, people are not often moved by general and theoretical exhortations. Rather we respond more readily to concrete arguments directed toward specific situations. That is why it would be futile merely to reiterate that we need more responsibility for others and for ourselves. Instead, this book has offered definite approaches on specific issues, to advance that end. The chosen issues relate to the most basic right, the right to life itself. If people cannot be moved on these issues, they are not likely to be moved on any other. Moreover, the selected issues discussed in this book have a unifying factor beyond their concern with the right to live. For each one involves in a special way an abdication of responsibility for others and an evasion of accountability for one's own acts. Also, when we put them all together, we can picture an ominous future.

Artificial insemination, for example, shows the potential for abuse latent in a science uninformed by a coherent respect for life. Science has given man the power to play God, in the capacity to construct human beings on order, to produce them according to a recipe much as one would produce various cookies or cupcakes by changing the recipe. Artificial insemination could be used by a total state to produce human beings on order, with a potential that is nothing short of dehumanizing. Also, there is the evident avoidance of responsibility by donors for the children they have artificially sired and a similar evasion by the donor of accountability for his act of vicarious procreation.

Artificial insemination could be seriously considered as a human engineering technique only in a society that had lost its reverence for life. Only when life is regarded as cheap rather than precious, as a thing to be manipulated rather than as a gift of God, could such a thing be possible. And yet the decay that can lead to a tolerance of artificial insemination has its origins elsewhere. When easy abortion, for example, is proposed as a humanitarian measure it brings in its train an active contempt for life. Also, when the mother procures the death of her own child, entrusted to her total protection and care, she spurns her responsibility to that child and escapes the consequences of her voluntary act of procreation. Even when the child was conceived by rape the hostility and irresponsibility to the child are manifest. We are on the verge of accepting abortion as a way of life in this country. If we do, we shall be able to raise no principled objection to its use at the whim of the mother or, worse still, at the command of public officials who will regard it as merely another technique for the advancement of the welfare of the state.

Abortion, moreover, is no different in principle from euthanasia. Whether voluntary or involuntary, the practice of euthanasia is wholly inconsistent with a proper reverence for life. The Nazi use of involuntary euthanasia was designed to rid the Third Reich of Jews and other "useless eaters." Its employment by our contemporary humanitarians would be couched in different terms but would be equally pernicious in principle. Further, there is a built-in tendency for the voluntary type, urged in bland and merciful tones, to degenerate inevitably into the involuntary. Either type is indefensible in principle and it is no less so in effect. Both must be resisted.

After discussing euthanasia, we moved into a treatment of suicide. Voluntary euthanasia can be rejected because a decision to die on the part of a terminal patient is inherently unreliable. But suicide is also wrong, even assuming that the suicide's decision was wholly voluntary and even rational. There is no great danger that there will be a mass epidemic of suicides. However, the growth of a distorted attitude in this area can retard the development of a due regard for life in other matters. Suicide involves an evasion of responsibility but its ultimate rejection depends upon the fact that it is an affront to God. All the other issues treated in this book can be disposed of on essentially secular grounds. But the only way one can say that suicide is always wrong is to base that position on a supernatural foundation. Yet this foundation is important for all these issues. Although we do not have to rely on God's injunction to reject abortion, euthanasia, or unrestrained contraception, only a theistic belief can generate an adequate realization of the need for a restoration of responsibility. However, a belief in God is more than merely a useful tool in this effort. For God does exist in fact. His will, therefore, must be done as fully as we can find it and do it.

We are not claiming, however, that the right to life is absolute. Its sanctity does not preclude its forfeitability. Justice Holmes once said that the right to swing your fist stops just short of the other man's nose. And so it is with the right to live. Indeed that right is so important that it merits the ultimate sanction in its enforcement. To advocate capital punishment is easy when one is not the star performer in the execution. And clearly the power of the state to impose the ultimate penalty must be restricted with safeguards. But to deny that power could only cheapen innocent life by removing a protection that, to some extent, does uniquely deter some homicides and therefore does save some innocent lives. Unfortunately some critics couple their opposition to the death penalty with a virtual denial of general responsibility on the part of criminals for the crimes they commit. This tendency must be resisted while we carefully hedge about the power of life and death with protections against abuse. If, on the other hand, we deny that a murderer can forfeit his right to live, we jeopardize the lives of potential victims, we ultimately reduce murder to the status of an ordinary crime, and we seriously cheapen innocent life.

Contraception was covered next in this book because it shows the same irresponsible trends operating even before life has begun. Contraception is different from abortion, except so far as some contraceptive pills and devices are themselves abortifacients. But the irresponsibility inherent in the unrestrained practice of contraception is akin to that involved in killing the existing child in the womb or "mercifully" dispatching the elderly and infirm. Indeed, contraception in some ways is the most important issue treated in this book. In a society increasingly preoccupied with sex, the issue of responsibility in that area assumes a greater importance than in any other. If people will assume their responsibilities in matters of sex, they can be expected to assume them on other matters less important to the world today. If, however, people abdicate their responsibilities on contraception, we cannot be too surprised if they abdicate them on abortion and euthanasia, which terminate existing lives. Contraception, moreover, is at once both a symbolic and a very practical issue. If the contraceptive trend is not reversed, promiscuity will be even more rampant, the integrity of the family will be further compromised. and predictably the social engineers will claim the power to decide even who shall be born.

Similarly, sterilization is symbolic and practical. It is particularly important as a birth control measure. It is a permanent form of contraception and it is virtually foolproof as a preventive of births. But its tolerance would entail the same pernicious effects as would an acceptance of the more transient abdication involved in contraception.

In a real sense, contraception and sterilization are perversions. They deliberately separate the pleasurable from the creative in the use of the reproductive faculties. It is not surprising, therefore, that the Age of the Pill is also the Age of the Third Sex, with an evident increase of the overt perversion of homosexuality. We should strive for compassion toward the person afflicted with homosexual tendencies. But we cannot afford to ignore the necessity of restraining and, within limits, punishing the commission of homosexual acts in public or in private and regardless of the consent of the parties to those acts. If we can strengthen the public attitude in this area, if we can substitute the realistic for the blindly permissive, it will greatly help to reverse the over-all trend with which we are concerned.

The crisis of responsibility occasioned this book. It is a far-reaching crisis, extending beyond the few issues we have discussed here. But those issues are so important, involving as they do the very right to live, that a redirection of attitude on them could prompt a general reawakening of responsibility for others and of accountability for our own acts. This book is written in the hope that it might contribute toward that end. We are pursuing that end here by promoting the basic civil right to live. And the attainment of that end will be conducive to the enjoyment of liberty by all. For it is true that irresponsibility breeds license and repression. We are contending for a return to responsibility because liberty can only be secure when citizens observe their due responsibilities for others and when all are responsible for their voluntary acts. Nor is it incidental that the civil rights of women are particularly affected here. It is the woman whose right to bear children is questioned by those who would subordinate that right to the interest of the state. Easy abortion is advanced as a woman's natural right. But the attainment of such a right would be illusory and a prelude to the coercive limitation of that right and perhaps even to the denial of her right to have children at all. Similar considerations obtain in the areas of artificial insemination, contraception, and sterilization. Rather than a misleading appeal to a distorted feminism, we need a greater awareness that the civil rights of all are ultimately at stake.

In summary, the lesson of common sense and history is that liberty can be retained only if we are willing to assume our responsibilities under God. If we will not do it when the right to live itself is at stake, we will never do it. Instead we will consign ourselves to the total state. We will lose our right to live as well as our liberty. And we will deserve to lose them both.

NOTES

One THE PROBLEM

1. Colorado Revised Statutes Annotated, Secs. 40–2–50 to 52 (Supp. 1967).
2. New York *Times*, March 12, 1965, p. 35, col. 3.
3. People v. Defore, 242 New York 13, 21 (1926).
4. See statement by Senator John L. McClellan, Congressional Record, February 23, 1967, S2494.
5. New York *News*, June 16, 1967, p. 78, col. 1.
6. *The Tablet*, November 21, 1960, p. 7, col. 1.
7. 2 Calvin's Case, 7 Coke's Rep. 12 (a), 77 Eng. Rep. 392; see discussion in Natural Law Institute Proceedings (1947), p. 8.
8. Perry, *Sources of Our Liberties* (1959), p. 287.
9. Ibid., p. 339.
10. See Mietus, *The Therapeutic Abortion Act—A Statement in Opposition* (1967), p. 19.

Two ARTIFICIAL INSEMINATION

1. Gursky v. Gursky, 242 N.Y.S. 2d 406 (Sup. Ct., 1963).
2. People v. Sorensen, 62 Cal. Rep. 462, 465 (1967).
3. See generally, Rice, "AID: An Heir of Controversy," 34 *Notre Dame Lawyer* 510 (1959).
4. See New York *Times*, April 5, 1952, p. 18, col. 1.
5. See note, "Legal and Social Implications of Artificial Insemination," 34 *Iowa Law Review* 658 (1949).
6. See comment, "Parent & Child: Legal Effect of Artificial Insemination," 19 *Oklahoma Law Review* 448 (1966); *Medical-Moral Newsletter*, February–March 1968.
7. *Time*, February 25, 1966, p. 48.
8. Ibid.
9. See Puxon, "Without Father Bred," 102 *Solicitor's Journal* 95 (1958).

10. Orford v. Orford, 49 *Ontario Law Reports* 15, 58 *Dominion Law Reports* 251, 258 (1921).
11. Hoch v. Hoch (Unreported, Circuit Court of Cook County, Illinois, 1945); see Chicago *Sun*, February 10, 1945, p. 13, col. 3; *Time*, February 26, 1945, p. 58.
12. Strnad v. Strnad, 190 Misc. 786, 78 N.Y.S. 2d 390 (Sup. Ct. 1948).
13. Doornbos v. Doornbos (Unreported, No. 54 S. 14981); (Superior Ct., Cook Co., December 13, 1954), 23 U.S. Law Week 2308.
14. 12 Ill. App. 2nd, 473 (1955).
15. Bartholomew, "Legal Implications of Artificial Insemination," 21 *Modern Law Review* 236 (1958).
16. See Goldfarb, "Artificial Insemination—The Legal Viewpoint," 7 *Syracuse Law Review* 108 (1955).
17. See note, 32 *Washington Law Review* 280 (1957).
18. Haman, "Results in Artificial Insemination," 72 *Journal of Urology* 557 (1954).
19. Oklahoma Session Laws, 1967, Ch. 305.
20. See New York *Times*, May 5, 1967, p. 25, col. 5.
21. Weisman, "Artificial Insemination: The Medical Viewpoint," 7 *Syracuse Law Review* 96 (1956).
22. Mangin, "Artificial Insemination: The Sociological and Anthropological Viewpoint," 7 *Syracuse Law Review* 106 (1956).
23. *Morals and Medicine* (1954), pp. 103–4.
24. Bohn, "Artificial Insemination: Psychologic and Psychiatric Evaluation," 34 *University of Detroit Law Journal* 397 (1957).
25. Lang, "Artificial Insemination—Legitimate or Illegitimate?" *McCall's*, May 1955, pp. 33, 62.
26. Hahlo, "Some Legal Aspects of Human Artificial Insemination," 74 *South African Law Journal* 167 (1957).
27. Ibid.
28. See Bezzant, "Artificial Human Insemination," *The Fortnightly*, February 1949, p. 78.
29. See Ryan, "Artificial Insemination: The Religious Viewpoints," 7 *Syracuse Law Review* 99, 101 (1955).
30. New York *News*, December 15, 1967, p. 4, col. 1.
31. Ibid.
32. Koerner, "Medicolegal Considerations in Artificial Insemination," 8 *Louisiana Law Review* 484, 485 (1948).
33. See Muller, "Means and Aims in Human Genetic Betterment," in Sonneborn, *Control of Human Heredity and Evolution* (1965); see discussion in Ruggiero, "Genetic Selection and Human Dignity," *Catholic Mind*, February 1967, p. 32.
34. Guttmacher, "The Role of Artificial Insemination in the Treatment of Human Sterility," 19 *Bulletin* of the New York Academy of Medicine 576 (1943).

Notes

35. Kelly, "Artificial Insemination: Theological and Natural Law Aspects," 33 *University of Detroit Law Journal* 135, 144 (1955).

36. Ibid.

37. For a general discussion see Tyler, "The Control of Unborn Life," *Today's Health,* July 1966, p. 60.

38. See Los Angeles *Times,* January 21, 1968, p. 1, col. 3.

39. George Orwell, *1984* (1952), p. 52.

Three ABORTION

1. *Time,* February 25, 1966, p. 86.
2. Model Penal Code, Proposed Official Draft, Sec. 203.3 (1962).
3. Colo. Rev. Stat. Ann., Secs. 40–2–50 to 40–2–52 (Supp. 1967).
4. North Carolina Gen. Stat., Sec. 14–46 (Supp. 1967).
5. California Health and Safety Code, Secs. 25950–54 (Supp. 1967).
6. New York *Times,* June 16, 1967, p. 24, col. 3.
7. Elizabeth II, 1967, Ch. 87.
8. See Mietus, *The Therapeutic Abortion Act: A Statement in Opposition* (1967), pp. 2–6.
9. See Blumenthal, "Abortion Law Controversy," *Commentator* (New York University Law Center, September 13, 1967, p. 1).
10. *Twin Circle,* February 25, 1968, p. 2, col. 4.
11. Patten, *Human Embryology* (1964), pp. 35, 82; see also Patten, *Human Embryology* (1953), p. 54.
12. Patten, *Human Embryology* (1964), p. 79.
13. Ibid., p. 3.
14. Ruch, *Psychology and Life* (1963), p. 33.
15. Ratner, *A Doctor Talks about Abortion,* pp. 2–3.
16. A recording of such heartbeats, entitled "The Ultrasonic Sounds of Pregnancy," is available from Smith Kline Instrument Co., 1500 Spring Garden Street, Philadelphia, Pa. 19101.
17. See Mietus, op. cit., p. 16.
18. See "Drama of Life Before Birth," *Life,* April 30, 1965.
19. *Newsweek,* October 25, 1965, p. 67.
20. Beck, "Guarding the Unborn," *Today's Health,* January 1968, pp. 38, 40.
21. See the proposed Blumenthal-Dominick bill in the New York State legislature, A. 761, S.529 (Prefiled, January 3, 1968).
22. Conniff, "The World of the Unborn," New York *Times Magazine,* January 8, 1967, p. 41.
23. New York *News,* September 27, 1967, p. 4.
24. Furlong, "It's a Long Way from the Birds and Bees," New York *Times Magazine,* June 11, 1967, pp. 24, 25.
25. See Ratner, "Is It A Person or a Thing?" *Report,* April 1966, pp. 20, 22.
26. Smith v. Brennan, 31 N.J. 353, 362, 157 A. 2d 497, 502 (1960).

179

27. Kelly v. Gregory, 282 App. Div. 542, 544, 545 (3rd Dept., 1953).

28. Bonbrest v. Kotz, 65 F. Supp. 138, 140 (D. C. Dist. Col., 1946); see the subsequent authorities collected in Byrne, "A Critical Look at Legalized Abortion," 41 *Los Angeles Bar Bulletin* 320 (1966).

29. Prosser, *The Law of Torts* (1964), p. 355.

30. See Byrne, "A Critical Look at Legalized Abortion," *Los Angeles Bar Bulletin*, May 1966, pp. 320, 322; Prosser, *The Law of Torts* (1964), p. 357.

31. 42 N.J., 421, 201 A. 2d 537, cert. denied, 377 U.S. 985 (1965).

32. 201 A. 2d at 538.

33. Gleitman v. Cosgrove, 49 N.J. 22, 227 A. 2d 689, 693 (1967).

34. 227 A. 2d at 693.

35. Declaration of Rights of the Child, adopted by General Assembly of the United Nations, November 20, 1959.

36. See Daly, *Morals, Law and Life* (1966), p. 137.

37. Letter from Presiding Judge Barnett to Mrs. Sylvia Bloom, Association for the Study of Abortion, Inc., 120 West 57th Street, New York, N.Y., December 22, 1967; see Los Angeles *Herald-Examiner*, December 8, 1967, p. A. 20, col. 1.

38. Testimony of Dr. Morris S. Fond on behalf of United Synagogue of America and other agencies, Joint Hearings of Health and Codes Committees, New York, N.Y., February 10, 1967.

39. Fletcher, *Situation Ethics* (1966), p. 39.

40. American Law Institute, Model Penal Code (Tentative Draft No. 8) (1958) p. 1, 16–17. (Emphasis added.)

41. See, *Long Island Catholic*, March 21, 1968, p. 10, col. 2; Proceedings of National Meeting of Diocesan Attorneys, April 1967 (United States Catholic Conference, Washington, D.C.), pp. 32–42.

42. Byrn, "Abortion in Perspective," 5 *Duquesne Law Review* 125, 140 (1966); see also Shaw, "Abortion and Public Policy" (National Catholic Welfare Conference, 1966).

43. Ratner, "Medical Implications of the Current Abortion Law in Illinois," *Illinois Medical Journal*, May 1967, pp. 687, 689.

44. See Calderone, *Abortion in the United States* (1958), pp. 36–37; Byrn, op. cit.

45. See New York *Times*, January 8, 1968, p. 28, col. 1.

46. See *Medical-Moral Newsletter*, March 1967.

47. New York *News*, March 1, 1968, p. 38, col. 1.

48. New York *Times*, December 14, 1967, p. 56, col. 1; Lear, "The Second Feminist Wave," New York *Times Magazine*, March 10, 1968, p. 24.

49. Policy Statement on Abortion Laws, 1968, American Civil Liberties Union, 156 Fifth Ave., New York, N.Y. 10010.

50. See Diamond, "The Doctor's Case Against Freer Abortion Laws," *Report*, February 1967, p. 28.

51. See Ryan, "Liberalized Abortion Laws—Immoral and Dangerous," *New York Law Journal*, April 19, 1966.

52. *Long Island Catholic*, February 23, 1967.

53. See Ratner, "Medical Implications of the Current Abortion Law in Illinois," pp. 687, 692.

54. See discussion in pastoral letter by Bishop Fulton J. Sheen, *The Tablet*, March 2, 1967.

55. See Mietus, op. cit., p. 16.

56. Birmingham *Evening Mail and Despatch*, October 13, 1966.

57. Guttmacher, "Techniques of Therapeutic Abortion," *Clinical Obstetrics and Gynecology*, March 1964, pp. 100, 103. (Emphasis added.)

58. See London *Daily Telegraph*, June 2, 1967.

59. *Maryknoll Magazine*, April 1965.

60. *Medical-Moral Newsletter*, June 1966.

61. Ibid., January 1967; New York *News*, January 6, 1968, p. 10, col. 5.

62. Jakobovits, "Jewish Views on Abortion," 17 *Western Reserve Law Review* 480, 487 (1965).

63. Birmingham *Evening Mail and Despatch*, October 13, 1966. (Emphasis in original.)

64. *Twin Circle*, February 11, 1968. (Emphasis in original.)

65. Quay, "Justifiable Abortion," 40 *Georgetown Law Journal* 173, 446 (1961).

66. See Mietus, op. cit., p. 52.

67. Hall, "Thalidomide and Our Abortion Laws," *Columbia University Forum*, Vol. VI, pp. 10, 13 (1963).

68. Ratner, "Medical Implications of the Current Abortion Law in Illinois," *Illinois Medical Journal*, pp. 687, 690.

69. New York *Times*, February 21, 1968, p. 51, col. 1.

70. *Medical-Moral Newsletter*, February–March 1968.

71. Hellegers, *A Doctor Looks at Abortion*, p. 4. (Emphasis in original.)

72. *Twin Circle*, February 11, 1968, p. 8, col. 1.

73. New York *Times*, January 8, 1968, p. 28, col. 1.

74. *Twin Circle*, February 11, 1968, p. 8, col. 1.

75. Marks and Paperno, *New York Criminal Law* (1961), Sec. 85.

76. See Ratner, "The Rock Book: A Catholic Viewpoint," *Commonweal*, July 5, 1963.

77. *Yearbook of Obstetrics and Gynecology* (1940), p. 69; see Ratner, *Abortion: A Public Health Viewpoint*, p. 20.

Four   EUTHANASIA

1. Repouille v. U.S., 165 F. 2d 152, 153 (2d Cir., 1947).

2. Williams, *The Sanctity of Life and the Criminal Law* (1957), p. 340.

3. Ibid.

4. See Silving, "Euthanasia: A Study in Comparative Criminal Law," 103 *University of Pennsylvania Law Review* 350, 386 (1954).

5. See Kamisar, "Some Non-Religious Views Against Proposed 'Mercy-Killing' Legislation," 42 *Minnesota Law Review* 969 (1958).

6. See cases collected in Annotation, "Testamentary Capacity as Affected by Use of Intoxicating Liquor or Drugs," 9 *American Law Reports* 3rd 15 (1966).

7. Frohman, "Vexing Problems in Forensic Medicine: A Physician's View," 31 *New York University Law Review* 1215, 1221 (1956). (Emphasis in original.)

8. See Taylor, "Annotations on the Oath of Hippocrates and the Geneva Version of the Hippocratic Oath," 23 *Linacre Quarterly* 34 (1956); see Note, 34 *Notre Dame Lawyer* 460 (1959).

9. Frohman, op. cit.

10. See Williams, "Euthanasia and Abortion," 38 *University of Colorado Law Review* 178, 186 (1966).

11. 169 H. L. Deb. 551, 559 (1950); see discussion in Kamisar, op. cit., 1016.

12. Williams, "Euthanasia and Abortion."

13. Arendt, *Eichmann in Jerusalem* (1965), p. 106; see also Reitlinger, *The Final Solution* (Perpetua ed., 1961).

14. See *Trials of War Criminals Before the Nuernberg Military Tribunals*, Vol. I ("The Medical Case"), p. 795.

15. See Wertham, *A Sign for Cain* (1966), pp. 165–66.

16. *Trials*, Vol. I, p. 893.

17. Ibid., p. 880.

18. Quoted in Mitscherlick and Mielke, *Doctors of Infamy* (1949), p. 103; see Kamisar, op. cit. 1032.

19. Wertham, op. cit., p. 159.

20. *Trials*, Vol. I, p. 880.

21. Alexander, "Medical Science Under Dictatorship," 241 *New England Journal of Medicine* 39, 40 (1949); see Kamisar, op. cit., 1031–32. (Emphasis in original.)

22. *Trials*, Vol. I, pp. 866–67.

23. Ibid., p. 801.

24. Affidavit of Defendant Brock, ibid., p. 844.

25. Ibid., p. 801.

26. Ibid., p. 796.

27. Ibid., pp. 865–70.

28. *Catholic Worker*, November 1967, p. 4.

29. Statement of Prosecutor, *Trials*, Vol. I, p. 71.

30. Wertham, op. cit., pp. 183–84.

31. See ibid., Chaps. 8 and 9.

32. Affidavit of Defendant Brock, *Trials*, Vol. I, p. 844.

33. Ibid., p. 69.

34. See *Facts on Communism*, Vol. II, U. S. Government Printing Office (1960), pp. 159–65.

35. *National Review Bulletin*, January 9, 1968, p. B6.

Notes

36. Quoted in *Long Island Press*, November 8, 1967, p. 17, col. 4.
37. See *New York Times*, November 25, 1957; Note, 34 *Notre Dame Lawyer* 460 (1959).
38. *New York Times*, September 24, 1967, p. 1, col. 2.
39. Ibid., September 24, 1967, p. 1, col. 2; see also *Long Island Press*, November 8, 1967, p. 17, col. 6.
40. Address of February 24, 1957; see St. John-Stevas, *Life, Death and the Law* (1961), pp. 272–73.
41. Transcript, *The Gift of Life and the Right to Die*, Public Broadcast Laboratory, January 21, 1968, p. 6.
42. See *New York Times*, December 10, 1967, p. 63, col. 1.
43. See discussion in Goodman, "Doctors Must Experiment on Humans," *New York Times Magazine*, July 2, 1967, p. 12.
44. See Hyman v. Jewish Chronic Disease Hospital, 15 N.Y. 2nd 338 (1965).
45. See *Trials*, Vol. II, pp. 181–84.
46. See Barber, "Experimenting with Humans," *The Public Interest*, Winter 1967, p. 91.
47. See Freund, "Is the Law Ready for Human Experimentation?" *Trial*, October–November 1966, p. 46.

Five SUICIDE

1. *New York News*, February 12, 1968, p. 2, col. 1; ibid., February 13, 1968, p. 10, col. 1; *New York Post*, February 12, 1968, p. 2, col. 5.
2. *World Almanac* (1968), p. 895.
3. *Historical Statistics of the United States* (1957), p. 26.
4. *New York Times*, December 11, 1966, p. 144, col. 3.
5. Ibid., January 21, 1968, p. 46, col. 3.
6. *Statistical Abstract of the United States* (1965), p. 162.
7. *World Almanac* (1968), p. 49.
8. Palmer, *The Lengthening Shadow of Suicide* (Claretian Publications, 1965), p. 4.
9. 1 Hale, Pleas of the Crown 411; see discussion in Clark and Marshall, *A Treatise on the Law of Crimes* (1967), p. 623.
10. Myrdal, "The Swedish Way to Happiness," *New York Times Magazine*, January 30, 1966, p. 14. (The last penal sanctions against suicide were repealed in England in 1962.)
11. See Commonwealth v. Mink, 123 Mass. 422, 426, 25 Am. Rep. 109 (1877).
12. See Shipman v. Protected Home Circle, 174 N.Y. 398, 410 (1903); Litman, "Medical-Legal Aspects of Suicide," 6 *Washburn Law Journal* 395 (1967).
13. See Williams, *The Sanctity of Life and the Criminal Law* (1957), pp. 288–89.
14. Shneidman and Mandelkorn, *How to Prevent Suicide* (Public Affairs Committee, Inc., 1967), p. 8.
15. Durkheim, *Suicide* (1952).

16. See Hendin, *Suicide and Scandinavia* (1965), pp. 78–79; Evans and Moore, *The Lawbreakers* (1968), pp. 183–88.

17. Palmer, op. cit., p. 5.

18. *Nicomachean Ethics* (Thomson trans., 1953), Vol. III, p. 8.

19. Boston *Pilot*, June 20, 1964.

20. Blackstone, *Commentaries* (4th ed., 1899), Vol. IV, p. 189.

21. *Triumph*, June 1967, p. 8.

22. See Stengel and Cook, "Recent Research into Suicide and Attempted Suicide," 1 *Journal of Forensic Medicine* 252 (1954).

23. Shneidman and Mandelkorn, op. cit., p. 5.

24. See New York Penal Law, Sec. 35.10 (4).

25. See "Annotation," 9 *American Law Reports* 3rd 1391 (1966). The courts generally hold that medical treatment of a child can be ordered by the public authority where necessary to save his life, despite the objections of the parents.

26. *Hamlet*, Act I, Scene 2.

27. Litman, "Medical-Legal Aspects of Suicide," 6 *Washburn Law Journal* 395, 396 (1967).

28. Plato, *Dialogues of Phaedo*.

Six   CAPITAL PUNISHMENT

1. See New York *News*, January 21, 1968, p. 86.

2. New York *Times*, February 15, 1968, p. 35, col. 1.

3. Ibid., May 10, 1967, p. 34, col. 1.

4. *U. S. News & World Report*, April 10, 1967, p. 72.

5. Ibid.

6. New York *Times*, February 15, 1968, p. 35, col. 1.

7. *Long Island Catholic*, February 15, 1968, p. 18, col. 7.

8. St. John-Stevas, *The Right to Life* (1963), p. 81.

9. Favreau, *Capital Punishment* (1965), pp. 8–9.

10. Toland, "Sad Ballad of the Real Bonnie and Clyde," New York *Times Magazine*, February 18, 1968, pp. 26, 28.

11. *U. S. News & World Report*, April 10, 1967, p. 72.

12. Favreau, op. cit., pp. 52, 53.

13. Ibid., p. 125.

14. Ibid., p. 59.

15. Ibid., p. 54.

16. *Long Island Catholic*, June 10, 1965.

17. Favreau, op. cit., p. 50.

18. Ibid., p. 47.

19. New York *Journal-American*, March 26, 1965.

20. Ibid.

21. Favreau, op. cit., p. 14.
22. *Long Island Catholic*, June 10, 1965.
23. Favreau, op. cit., p. 46.
24. Ibid., p. 48.
25. Ibid., p. 6.
26. Kugelmass, "Dateline: Death House," *Our Sunday Visitor*, February 25, 1968, p. 4.
27. New York *News*, March 4, 1968, p. 3, col. 1.
28. Report, Sentencing Alternatives and Procedures, Advisory Committee on Sentencing and Review, American Bar Association (Tentative Draft, 1967), pp. 20, 130.
29. *U. S. News & World Report*, April 10, 1967, p. 72.
30. Favreau, op. cit., p. 83.
31. New York *Times*, March 14, 1968, p. 38, col. 3.
32. Miranda v. Arizona, 384 U.S. 436 (1966).
33. See 384 U.S. at 521–23.
34. New York *Times*, April 20, 1967.
35. Mallory v. United States, 354 U.S. 449 (1957).
36. Public Law 90–226, Sec. 301.
37. Public Law 90–351.
38. See *Human Events*, February 4, 1967, p. 8.
39. See New York Penal Law, Secs. 125. 30, 125. 35.
40. See Report, Appellate Review of Sentences, Advisory Committee on Sentencing and Review, American Bar Association (Tentative Draft, 1967), p. 31.

Seven CONTRACEPTION

1. New York *Times*, March 10, 1968, p. E5. (Emphasis in original throughout.)
2. Ibid., March 11, 1968, p. 43, col. 1.
3. *U. S. News & World Report*, October 4, 1965, p. 54.
4. Paper prepared by Barbara Ward for meeting of Oxford Committee for Famine Relief, July 30–August 5, 1963, p. 2; see *Christopher News Notes*, June–July 1964.
5. *Medical-Moral Newsletter*, May 1967.
6. Carter, "Are Population 'Experts' Running Wild?" *Our Sunday Visitor*, May 16, 1965, p. 1.
7. New York *Times*, March 10, 1968, p. 74, col. 1.
8. First National City Bank, *Monthly Economic Letter*, September 1967, p. 107.
9. New York *Times*, December 24, 1965.
10. First National City Bank, op. cit., p. 106.
11. Carter, op. cit., p. 1, col. 1.
12. New York *News*, September 17, 1967.

13. Ibid., March 17, 1968, p. 52, col. 1.
14. *The Soul*, 30.4; quoted in Noonan, *Contraception* (1965), p. 83.
15. *Against Helvidius* 21, PL 23:215; quoted in Noonan, op. cit.
16. Statement of Administrative Board, National Catholic Welfare Conference, *The Tablet*, November 28, 1959.
17. New York *News*, June 29, 1967, p. 3, col. 1; U. S. *News & World Report*, April 17, 1967, p. 48; New York *Times*, February 26, 1968, p. 1, col. 2; U. S. *News & World Report*, March 11, 1968, p. 57.
18. *Medical-Moral Newsletter*, May 1966.
19. Ibid., November 1966.
20. U. S. *News & World Report*, March 11, 1968, p. 59.
21. New York *Times*, October 4, 1967.
22. Ibid., September 30, 1967.
23. New York *News*, August 15, 1967, p. 2, col. 2.
24. Ibid., January 6, 1968, p. 21. (Emphasis in original.)
25. Ibid., December 13, 1967, p. 4, col. 1.
26. New York *Times*, January 15, 1968, p. 11, col. 3.
27. Ibid., April 30, 1967, p. 26, col. 1.
28. Ibid., February 23, 1968, p. 12, col. 3.
29. See U. S. *News & World Report*, June 12, 1967, p. 64.
30. *The Tablet*, August 19, 1965.
31. U. S. *News & World Report*, March 11, 1968, p. 59.
32. New York *Times*, March 24, 1968, p. 14, col. 1.
33. *Long Island Catholic*, January 31, 1963.
34. Ibid., October 14, 1964.
35. U. S. *News & World Report*, October 4, 1965, p. 55.
36. New York *Times*, December 12, 1967, p. 1, col. 3.
37. Ibid., April 16, 1967, p. 1, col. 5; New York *Times*, August 1, 1968, p. 28, col. 4.
38. *Medical-Moral Newsletter*, September 1966.
39. *The Wanderer*, December 14, 1967, p. 3, col. 4.
40. New York *World Journal Tribune*, April 16, 1967.
41. New York *Times*, April 11, 1967.
42. Ibid., May 11, 1968, p. 36, col. 3; Washington *Post*, May 1, 1968, p. A3, col. 6.
43. New York *World Journal Tribune*, April 23, 1967, p. 19, col. 1.
44. New York *Times*, May 23, 1967, p. 28, col. 2.
45. *Medical-Moral Newsletter*, June 1967.
46. Ibid., May 1966.
47. Ibid., June 1967.
48. Ibid., October 1966.
49. U. S. *News & World Report*, February 5, 1968, p. 10.

50. New York *Times*, May 7, 1967, p. 43, col. 1.

51. Ibid., January 22, 1968, p. 1, col. 2.

52. *Medical-Moral Newsletter*, June 1967.

53. New York *Times*, November 18, 1967, p. 1, col. 8.

54. Ibid., April 12, 1967, p. 1, col. 7.

55. Acta Apostolicae Sedis, 43 (1951), 843, see Kelly, *Christian Unity and Christian Marriage* (Family Life Bureau, National Catholic Welfare Conference, March 1964), p. 11.

56. *The Wanderer*, November 10, 1966.

57. New York *Times*, July 30, 1968, p. 20, col. 4 (from text of Pope Paul VI's encyclical of July 29, 1968, *Humanae Vitae*).

58. See generally, Von Hildebrand, *Morality and Situation Ethics* (1966); Fletcher, *Situation Ethics* (1966).

59. Newman, *The Idea of a University* (1959), p. 360.

60. See discussion in Daly, *Morals, Law and Life* (1966), p. 115.

61. *McCall's*, October 1967, p. 46.

62. Ibid., p. 150.

63. *Medical-Moral Newsletter*, April 1967.

64. New York *Times*, March 14, 1968, p. 20, col. 3.

65. See *Medical Tribune*, October 3, 1966.

66. *Medical-Moral Newsletter*, March 1967.

67. *Medical World News*, April 29, 1966.

68. *Medical-Moral Newsletter*, March 1967.

69. New York *News*, August 6, 1967.

70. *The Wanderer*, May 18, 1967, p. 1, col. 1.

71. Daly, op. cit., p. 45.

72. Ibid., pp. 94–95.

73. New York *Times*, April 7, 1967, p. 39, col. 4.

74. Ibid., November 13, 1967; *Science*, November 10, 1967; *Medical-Moral Newsletter*, December 1967.

75. Denver *Register*, May 11, 1967; *The Wanderer*, May 18, 1967.

76. *Medical-Moral Newsletter*, February–March 1968.

77. See Evans and Novak, "Inside Report," New York *Herald Tribune*, December 10, 1965.

78. See Ball, "Population Control: Civil and Constitutional Concerns," 1967 *Journal of Religion and Public Affairs* (Cornell University Press).

79. *Medical-Moral Newsletter*, March 1966.

80. Ibid., September–October 1967.

81. Ibid.

82. Ibid.

83. Ibid., April 1967.

84. New York *Times*, April 4, 1967; New York *World Journal Tribune*, April 18, 1967, p. 25.

85. *Medical-Moral Newsletter*, November 1966.

86. See discussion in Daly, op. cit., pp. 108–9.

87. *U. S. News & World Report*, March 11, 1968, p. 59.

88. New York *Times*, March 31, 1968, p. 28, col. 1.

89. *Child and Family*, Winter 1968, p. 13.

90. *McCall's*, October 1967.

91. *The Wanderer*, February 1, 1968.

92. Ibid., December 14, 1967, p. 3, col. 4.

93. *Summa Theologica*, 1–2, 96, 2; see Daly, op. cit., p. 22.

94. *Triumph*, July 1967, p. 8, New York *Times*, August 28, 1968.

95. See Griswold v. Connecticut, 381 U.S. 479 (1965); see "Griswold v. Connecticut; The Justices and Connecticut's Uncommonly Silly Law," 42 *Notre Dame Lawyer* 680 (1967).

96. See Note, "The History and Future of the Legal Battle over Birth Control," 49 *Cornell Law Quarterly* 275, 278 (1964).

97. *Newsday*, October 20, 1967, p. 3B, col. 1.

98. *Long Island Catholic*, May 9, 1963.

99. New York *Times*, March 4, 1968, p. 40, col. 1.

Eight STERILIZATION

1. Lelyveld, "It's God's Will. Why Interfere?" New York *Times Magazine*, January 14, 1968, p. 29.

2. Ibid.

3. See Comment, "Sterilization: A Continuing Controversy," 1 *University of San Francisco Law Review* 159, 161 (1966); Note, "Elective Sterilization," 113 *University of Pennsylvania Law Review* 415, 417 (1965).

4. See St. John-Stevas, *Life, Death and the Law* (1961), p. 160.

5. Note, "Elective Sterilization," 113 *University of Pennsylvania Law Review* 415, 416 (1965).

6. *Medical-Moral Newsletter*, April 1967.

7. See Association for Voluntary Sterilization, Inc., *The Physician and Contraceptive Sterilization*.

8. See comment, "Sterilization: A Continuing Controversy."

9. See 15 Syracuse Law Review 738, 739 (1964).

10. See Le Maire, "Danish Experiences Regarding the Castration of Sexual Offenders," 47 *Journal of Criminal Law Criminology and Police Science* 294 (1957); see 1 *University of San Francisco Law Review* 159, 173 (1966).

11. Skinner v. Oklahoma, 316 U.S. 535, 541 (1942).

12. See New York *Times*, April 21, 1968, p. 1, col. 3, and April 22, 1968, p. 43, col. 3.

13. *Medical-Moral Newsletter*, April 1967.

14. Buck v. Bell, 274 U.S. 200, 208 (1927).

15. 274 U.S. at 207.

16. See Bligh, "Sterilization and Mental Retardation," 51 *American Bar Association Journal* 1059 (1965).
17. See Goddard, *The Kallikak Family* (1912).
18. Sarason, *Psychological Problems in Mental Deficiency* (1959), p. 33.
19. Fernald, "The Feeble-Minded in the Community," *Social Aspects of Mental Hygiene* (1925), pp. 109–16.
20. Heiser, *Our Backward Children* (1955), p. 211.
21. Bligh, op. cit., p. 1065.
22. Extract from closing brief against defendant Rudolf Brandt, *Trials of War Criminals Before the Nuernberg Military Tribunals*, Vol. I, *The Medical Case*, pp. 695–96.
23. See *Long Island Catholic*, September 14, 1967.
24. New York *News*, September 26, 1966; see *Association for Voluntary Sterilization News*, Spring 1967, p. 1.
25. *Medical-Moral Newsletter*, April 1967.
26. Ibid.
27. New York *Times*, February 26, 1968, p. 14, col. 3.
28. Conn. Gen. Stat. Rev., Sec. 53–33 (1958); Utah Code Ann., Sec. 64–10–12 (1953).
29. Casti Connubli, December 31, 1930.
30. St. John-Stevas, *Life, Death and the Law*, op. cit., p. 187.
31. Fletcher, *Morals and Medicine* (1955), p. 168.
32. St. John-Stevas, *Life, Death and the Law*, op. cit., pp. 190–91.
33. See Association for Voluntary Sterilization, Statement of Purpose and Program (undated).

Nine HOMOSEXUALITY

1. Webster Schott, "A 4-Million Minority Asks for Equal Rights," New York *Times Magazine*, November 12, 1967, p. 44.
2. See Kinsey, Pomeroy and Martin, *Sexual Behavior in the Human Male* (1948).
3. Stearn, *The Sixth Man* (1962).
4. N. Y. Penal Law, Secs. 70.15, 130–38; Nevada Rev. Stat., Sec. 201–190.
5. *The Wolfenden Report* (1963), p. 27.
6. Ibid., pp. 28–29.
7. Ibid., p. 29.
8. Report of the Committee on Homosexual Offenses and Prostitution (1957), p. 24.
9. See Schott, op. cit., p. 44.
10. New York *Times*, May 3, 1967, p. 1, col. 1.
11. Ibid., May 4, 1967, p. E5, col. 1.
12. Schott, op. cit., p. 44.
13. See discussion in Schur, *Crimes without Victims* (1965), p. 89.

14. New York *Times*, December 3, 1967, p. E7, col. 4, and November 19, 1967.
15. Ibid., November 29, 1967, p. 1, col. 6.
16. John Stuart Mill, "On Liberty," Chap. 1.
17. See Hart, *Law, Liberty and Morality* (1963), pp. 31, 33.
18. *The Wolfenden Report*, p. 197.
19. Devlin, *The Enforcement of Morals* (1965), p. 14.
20. *The Wolfenden Report*, pp. 30–31.
21. Ibid., p. 33.
22. Ibid., p. 34.
23. Ibid., p. 35.
24. Caprio and Brenner, *Sexual Behavior* (1961), p. 114.
25. New York *Times Magazine*, January 28, 1968, p. 15 (Letter to the Editor).
26. *The Wolfenden Report*, pp. 40–41.
27. Ibid., p. 41.
28. Ibid., pp. 44–45.
29. Ibid., p. 192.
30. Ibid.
31. Ibid., pp. 194–98.
32. Ibid., p. 193.
33. 381 U.S. 479 (1965).
34. 381 U.S. at 485–86.
35. New York *Times*, March 3, 1966, p. 1, col. 2.
36. Abrams v. United States, 250 U.S. 616, 630 (1919) (dissenting opinion).
37. Letter to editor by Morton Friedman, M.D., New York *Times Magazine*, January 28, 1968, p. 15.
38. See Storr, *Sexual Deviation* (1964), Chap. 12, for a discussion of possible methods of treatment; see also Schur, op. cit., pp. 105–6.
39. New York *Times*, July 9, 1967, p. E7, col. 1.

INDEX

Index

Index

Hand, Judge Learned, 4, 52
Hanks, Nancy, 46
Häring, Rev. Bernard, 77–78
Harrison, Dr. J. Grant, 41
Health, Education and Welfare, Department of, 120, 124
Heckenholt Foundation, 64
Heffernan, Dr. R. J., 47
Hellegers, Dr. André, 47
Hernandez, Mrs. Nancy, 141
Herrings, birth rate of, 111
Himmler, Heinrich, 24, 150
Hippocrates, 50
Hippocratic Oath, 58
Hitler, Adolf, 12, 22, 28, 61–62, 64
Hoche, Alfred, 62
Hogan, Frank S., 101
Holmes, Dr. J. MacDonald, 119
Holmes, Justice Oliver Wendell, 147–48, 167, 171
Homosexuality, 6, 14, 154, 155–67, 173
Homosexuality, definition of, 155
Hoover, J. Edgar, 92
House of Lords, 53, 60
Humanae Vitae, 122, 152
Human Embryology, 29
Hungary, abortion in, 47
Hungary, suicide in, 41, 74
Huxley, Sir Julian, 24
Hysterectomy, 141
Hysterotomy, 42

Illegitimacy, 17, 25, 123
Illinois, 17, 30, 50, 113, 155–56, 162
Illinois, homosexuality in, 155–56, 162
Incest, 18, 26–29, 37–38
In Cold Blood (Capote), 91
India, 110–11, 113
India, Health Minister of, 113
India, population of, 110–11, 115
India, sterilization in, 113, 139, 150
Indiana, University of, 22
Indiana State Reformatory, 148
Indians, American, 111
Infanticide, 8, 44, 125
Inoculation, contraceptive, 12, 24
Institute of Human Development, 151
International Association for Voluntary Sterilization, 151
Intra-uterine devices, 113, 114, 120–21

Intra-uterine transfusion, 43
Ireland, 74, 117
Ishmaelite, treatment of defective as an, 149
Israel, 16

Jakobovits, Rabbi Immanuel, 23, 28, 44
Japan, 39, 41, 47, 117
Japan, abortions in, 39, 41, 43, 47, 114
Japan, birth rate in, 47, 114, 130
Japan, Health and Welfare Ministry of, 114
Japan, suicide in, 41
Java, Central, 113
Jerome, St., 111
Jersey City, 34
Jewish Chronic Disease Hospital, 71
"Jewish problem," Nazi "final solution to the," 8, 61
Jewish theologians, 21, 28
Jews, 21, 28, 46, 50, 62–63, 150, 171
John, King, 10
Johns Hopkins University, 47, 127, 128
Johnson, President Lyndon B., 22, 117
Judaeo-Christian morality, 157
Judaic civilization, 7
Jukes, 149

Kaiser Memorial Hospital, 35
Kallikaks, 149
Kearney, Judge Frank P., 142
Kelly, Monsignor George A., 133
Kentucky, University of, 118
Kew Gardens, New York, 2
Kidney machines, 69
Kings County, 15
Kinsey Report, 155
Knight, Mrs. Jill, 42, 45
Korea, 126
Kornberg, Arthur, 22
Kulaks, 65

Lady Family Planning Visitors, 113
Laidlaw, Robert W., 140
Lambeth Conference of 1930, 122
Lambeth Conference of 1958, 152
Landis, Prof. Judson, 151
Latin America, population of, 109
Law, Anglo-Saxon, 10

195

K21